The Seal of Liberty

America's Quest
for the
Lost Treasure of Freemasonry

Adam Schneider

Front cover description
Manhattan's Freedom Tower is perfectly aligned with the Emmet obelisk.
The tower ascends exactly **303** degrees from the obelisk. Emmet's bust looks
down Broadway, which bears exactly 33 degrees. The obelisk's longitude is
74°00'**33**.0" W, which is exactly 3-degrees east of the U.S. Capital Building.

Façade previously published in *Syncopated City* and *PoeTalk* journals.

Printed by CreateSpace

ISBN-13:
978-1517793821

ISBN-10:
1517793823

1) Social Science—Freemasonry; 2) History—United States; 3) Philosophy—Religious

www.sealofliberty.us

To my nephews:

Open-mindedness is the purest form of honesty—an admission of our unending ignorance.

Vector it with unending curiosity and bound it with reason, and you're on the path to discovery and wisdom.

Acknowledgements

I am grateful to my mother for her assistance in reviewing this text and for listening endlessly as I debated myself aloud. I hope that the reader possesses a portion of her tenacity, as the payoff of this work is revealed incrementally. My sister, my best friend, also provided helpful feedback.

I am indebted to my other reviewers, Joe F, Michael K, and Mike F. In addition to providing feedback on the text, they tolerated a lengthy presentation of the analytic material, which aimed to answer a simple question: Am I seeing ghosts here, or did I really discover a secret Freemason plan? I was comforted, having survived their doctorate-level scrutiny, that I was on the right path. Joe prompted the second part of the book, insisting that I seek to understand why Freemasons would undertake this effort. Technically focused, I didn't much care why, but I was rewarded by what I found.

All of my reviewers provided such thorough feedback that I can confidently conclude that any remaining errors or omissions are theirs, and theirs alone.

Every book of historic significance should begin with a poem. I wrote these words in 1993. Something about this book brought them to mind.

Parity

Good
and
Evil
meet
at
God
and
Love
and
Hate
and
are
only
differing
in
Sign.

Table of Contents

Prologue: A Secret Plan in Motion

Masonry should be an energy... bring[ing] forth from the man of enjoyments, the man of wisdom.

Masonry should not be a mere watch-tower, built upon mystery, from which to gaze at ease upon the world....

To hold the full cup of thought to the thirsty lips of men; to give to all the true ideas of Deity; to harmonize conscience and science, are the province of Philosophy.... Contemplation should lead to action....

Wisdom is a sacred communion.... the one and supreme method by which to unite Humanity and arouse it to concerted action.

Then Philosophy becomes Religion.

- Grand Commander of the Scottish Rite of Freemasonry (1871)

VVHAT TREASURE do you seek in life? Some seek material treasure, an amount of wealth that will empower them for a lifetime. Others seek spiritual treasure, a promise that a lifetime of just pursuits, moral behavior, or religious adherence will reward them with a blissful eternity after death. The symbols, rituals, and philosophy of Freemasonry are woven from both aspects of this quest for wealth, and no other secretive fraternity connects itself more with treasure than do the Freemasons. From its depictions in popular culture to its treatment in scholastic inquiries, Freemasonry seems *designed* to connect itself with a quest for that which is lost, no matter how powerful (Ark of the Covenant), material (Templar gold), spiritual (Holy Grail), or intellectual (original manuscripts of Shakespeare). What treasure does Freemasonry secretively protect that through its conspicuous placement of clues it entices us to seek?

Several hundred years ago, unknown persons undertook an ambitious effort to devise a complex philosophy and to create intricate rituals that narrate that philosophy. They masked their ideology behind layers of geometric, astrological, and religious symbols, and then they shrouded it all within a secret society. Why did these persons do this? The answer is not as frivolous as some would have you believe, nor is it as nefarious as the conspiracy theorists claim. The answer is no less important and no less ambitious and noble than the formation of a Land of Liberty. This book offers the first non-circumstantial evidence of a secret Freemason plan implemented in North America. George Washington, America's most famous Freemason, played an important and undeniable role in the implementation of this plan. *The Seal of Liberty* is unlike anything that you have previously read and reveals a systematic pattern of clues never before encountered.

Freemasons, particularly those of the Scottish Rite (33rd Degree), whether acting secretively within the Order or officially on its behalf, over the span of several hundred years and across hundreds of miles, deliberately constructed monuments, buildings, and city streets throughout the United States to conform to a single mathematically defined template, surrounded by recurring themes, and adhering to very accurate alignments among them. Together, these constructions form a larger picture, a map depicting two symbols, that is mathematically consistent with the template, and that is consistent with the symbols and purpose of the Order. This book guides the reader through the construction of this map and then uses the symbols and rituals of Freemasonry to decipher it, with little ambiguity. The creators of this map intended that it be considered a treasure map, although a related message is also clearly encoded within, which charts a path to the Land of the Free. For Washington and his collaborators, "liberty" has a deep meaning.

This book is not about a "conspiracy" and its methodology differs greatly from that used in conspiracy theories. Such theories sprout from an unwillingness to admit ignorance. They feed on faulty logic, tailored evidence, and shifting hypotheses, and they shelter within a fortress of bias. Often they are spurred by the weakest forms of speculation: "couldn't it be?" and "isn't it possible?" These are the lowest standards of reason, which demand equal consideration for irrational and unsupported ideas until they are proven to be impossible, which is impossible to do. But this book unquestionably reveals a secret plan. I use the term "secret plan," rather than "conspiracy," because conspiracies are inherently nefarious and this plan is not. Conspiracies aim to control and manipulate, whereas this plan articulates a choice, the defining attribute of Liberty. I came upon this plan while learning a specific type of mapping analysis, which I applied to disprove a conspiratorial claim that I saw on television. Soon, I encountered some curious phenomena that were hard to dismiss as coincidence. I developed a theory, tested it against the observable facts, and found it to be surprisingly predictive. After a thorough examination, I confidently declare that my theory is proven beyond all reasonable doubt. I do not cavalierly make such claims.

To veteran readers of the Freemason genre, this claim of a secret Freemason plan might not sound like anything new. Conspiracy theorists have been drawing Masonic symbols over the streets of Washington DC for ages. But, if you allow yourself a flexible template, as they do, then you can find patterns in clouds, see the Virgin Mary's face on a potato skin, or believe that Freemasons are hiding an alien civilization on Mars. Theirs is a revelation of bias, and nothing more. What's new here is the template, a mathematically defined structure that can be applied consistently and without alteration, and the alignments, which are not vague, but are precise and are tied to the dimensions of the template. Together, they form a very clear picture—a treasure map and a detailed and consistent symbolic narrative. *The Seal of Liberty* is the first quantifiable proof of a secret plan in motion, as compared to all other such claims that I am aware of, which rely entirely on dizzying amounts of circumstantial and speculative evidence. This plan must be unraveled as its ingenious creators intended, as a systematic quest for treasure. This book starts slowly, emphasizing technical details, and then builds quickly, taking sharp turns along the way. I ask the reader to join me on a quest to assemble and decipher this map, and to discover the long-hidden purpose of this plan.

I have deliberately kept this book lean. Rather than bewildering the reader with long-winded accounts of lineages and social networks, neither of which is my specialty (nor conclusive), I move quickly, albeit incrementally, through the quantifiable parts of the analysis. I produce for the reader a map, reveal the arrangements within it, and draw conclusions about the likelihood that these arrangements, in whole, are deliberate or coincidental. I also deduce from the arrangements a timeline of events. I then distill a large body of official Masonic literature down to portions relevant to deciphering the map. This distillation will reveal to the reader the core secrets of Freemasonry, from its secret philosophy to its deliberate deceptions—and the reasons for those deceptions. Surprisingly, a single plan is revealed that quantifiably ties Freemasonry to some of North America's most persistent mysteries, such as Oak Island and the Newport Tower.

I encourage the reader's evaluation of my analysis. In the appendices, I include all of my data and methods so that meticulous readers may attempt to reproduce, refute, or expand my findings. I also present in the appendices investigative leads and ideas that I left incomplete or unexplored.

Since this analysis is quantitative it relies heavily on numerical measures, mainly angles and distances. For those readers disinclined to tolerate these sorts of details, I ask that they consider this book's technical discussions not as tedious homework, but as an opportunity to add to their skill set an approach that can produce irrefutable conclusions. The numbers, though tedious to some, are not the bulk of the book, and are crucial. You will be rewarded for your patience. As you will see, in the end, these patterns undeniably exist and are too numerous, precise, and symbolically consistent to be dismissed as coincidence. No amount of circumstantial evidence can match this degree of certainty.

So, let's get started. The mathematically defined template that underpins this analysis is found on Oak Island. Yes, this is the same Oak Island that is famous for its spectacular claims of buried treasure and costly ends to which people have gone to unearth it. And that anchors this secret plan, as is common with Freemasonry, to a Quest for Treasure. So, we'll begin our quest there, on Oak Island, where men have been obliterating the landscape in search of material wealth since the time of George Washington's presidency.

Part I
Creating the Map

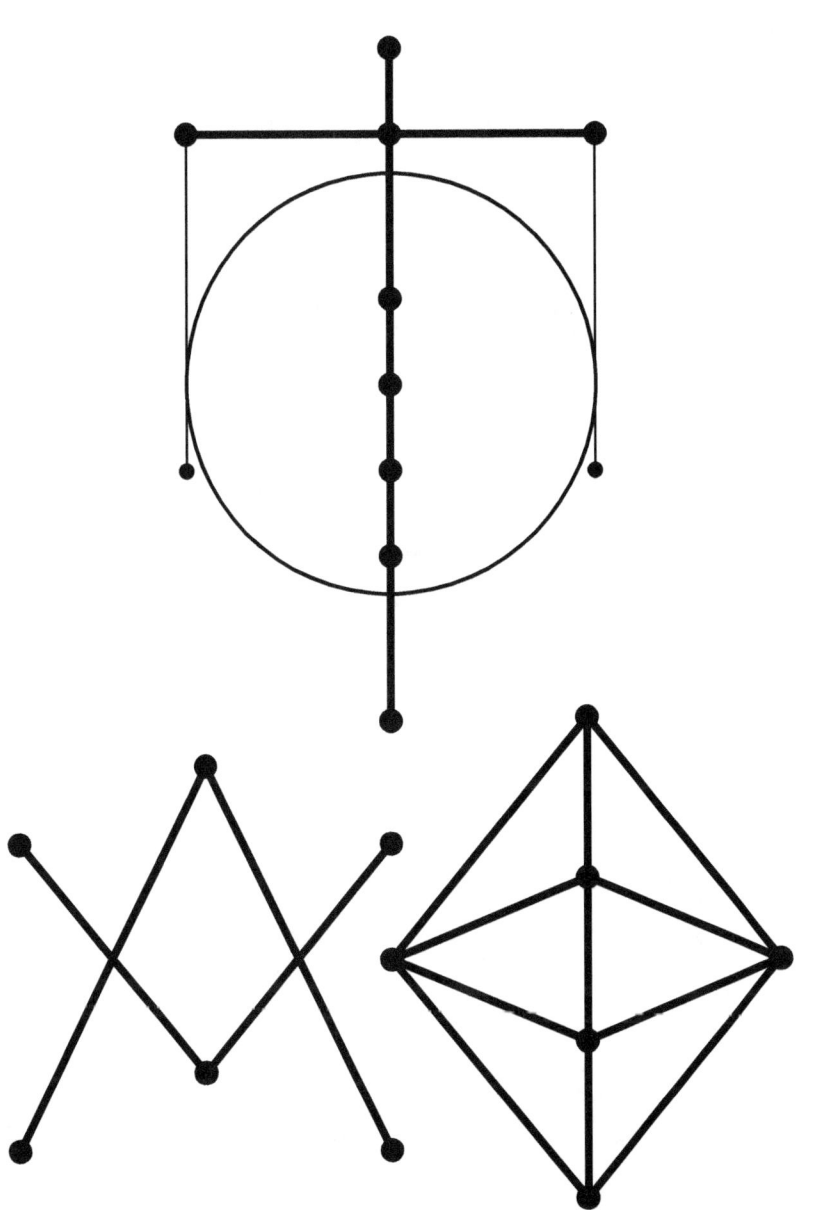

The Inferno and the Tree

The kingdom of heaven is like treasure hidden in a field. When a man
found it, he hid it again, and then in his joy went and sold all and bought
that field.[1]

- *Matthew* 13:44

In 1795, Daniel McGinnis, a nosy teenager, rowed a short distance from
mainland Nova Scotia (New Scotland) to a coastal island in Mahone Bay,
about 36 miles west-southwest of Halifax (see Figure 1). On the eastern end
of the island he discovered an odd scene. A large oak tree stood next to a
clearing among the trees. New trees were growing to replace those removed.
McGinnis noticed odd carvings in the trunk of the tall oak; one of its
branches had been forked and a triangular plug was inserted into the fork. A
tackle block was hung from this plug by rotten rope. McGinnis returned to
the mainland to solicit the help of two friends; one of them soon bought the
lot containing the clearing. The three friends attempted to retrieve the tackle
box, but it fell to the ground and broke easily. Its pieces collected into a
circular depression in the ground, as if loose dirt had settled and formed a
bowl about ten feet in diameter. McGinnis and his friends concluded that

---

[1] *Holy Bible: New International Version.* (1984). International Bible Society.

they had discovered the burial site of a pirate treasure. The site appeared to have been aged, perhaps decades old, with dirt settled, wood rotted, and new trees sprouted. This site, though, was not handled pristinely thereafter, as an archaeological dig, so any clues indicating its age and origin were quickly trampled or ignored by green-eyed men with digging tools in hand.

The three friends decided to dig in the depression and found at a depth of about two feet a floor of neatly placed stones not indigenous to the island. These stones, formed like a threshing floor (used to separate wheat from chaff), seemed to reveal the opening of a 13-foot diameter shaft, walls fortified by hard clay bearing visible pick marks. Digging more, at ten feet they found a platform made of oak logs. Soon, this hole became a shaft, revealing a new oak platform about every ten feet, for a total of nine platforms. For reasons that will become clear, I equate these nine platforms with the nine levels of Hell in Dante's *Inferno*. Eventually the pit filled with seawater, suggesting that its creators had fit the pit with a booby trap designed to protect its precious contents from treasure seekers. The "Money Pit" was born. Then, over the decades (and centuries) other shafts were dug and more clues, artifacts, booby traps, and disappointments were found. Freemasons were involved in these excavations, most notably Franklin Roosevelt (FDR) in 1909. By the 1960s large-scale heavy-machinery excavation of the island was underway. Photos from this time period, which are easily found on the Internet, reveal less of a treasure site than an industrial-scale quarry. Any subtle clues left on the island have long-since been steamrolled. Fortunately, the island has one not-so-subtle clue that partially remains.

In 1981, Oak Island resident, treasure hunter, and land surveyor Fred Nolan observed that a collection of large stones on the north side of the island was arranged in an apparently deliberate pattern. The stones were large cones, about 8-9 feet in the base and in height, and appeared set by man, as they were placed on crushed rocks and other materials to prevent sinking. Nothing about them matched their surrounding environment; they appeared clearly to be emplaced by humans and brought there from somewhere off the island. To Nolan, these stones, if connected by lines, seemed to collectively form the shape of a Christian cross with its vertical stem pointing toward the northeast. The formation is often called Nolan's Cross. One of the stones has a man-made carving of a face on it. It is a smaller stone with a flat bottom found shallowly buried at the intersection of the two lengths of the cross.

In 2002, Norwegian Rosecrucian and Shakespearian conspiracy theorist Petter Amundsen reflected on the shape of Nolan's Cross and concluded that it had the wrong dimensions and contained too many stones to be a cross (in the Christian sense) and that the spacing of the stones suggested another shape: a Qabalah Tree of Life (TOL).[2] Amundsen obtained the permission of one of the Oak Island landowners to survey the portions of the cross on their land and to search for stones that should be present if his Tree of Life theory was correct. Nolan did not grant similar access. So, in rainy conditions, armed with a shovel and a portable Global Positioning System (GPS) device, Amundsen obtained the geo-coordinates for several of the stones and uncovered two more stones that seemed to confirm his TOL theory.

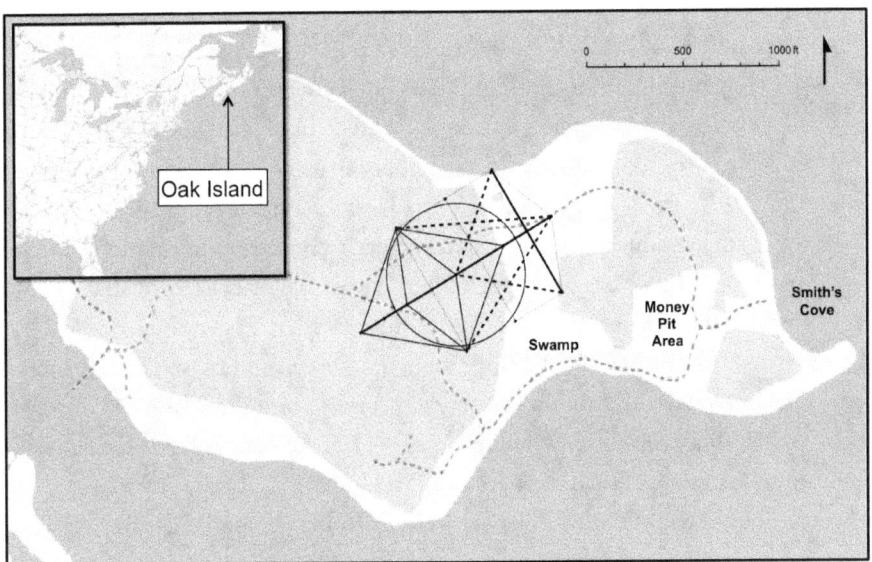

Figure 1: Oak Island and its Tree of Life

The bulk of the claims surrounding the Oak Island treasure, and even some of its less disputed historical recounts, seem dubious, as they rely heavily on unsubstantiated eyewitness accounts with key evidence being lost or stolen at every turn. Granted, the number and variety of eye-witnesses claiming to have observed evidence of a deep man-made burial on Oak Island would require a substantial conspiracy to fabricate, or a great deal of imagination-run-wild, or both. D'Arcy O'Connor, in his thorough examination of Oak Island concludes: "any suggestion that those three boys or their immediate successors launched a 210-year-old hoax is equally ridiculous, even without

---

[2] Amundsen, Petter. (2014) *Oak Island & the Treasure Map in Shakespeare*. Kindle Ed.

[modern] deep borehole discoveries." The existence of a deep refilled man-made hole seems without question, but the purpose and contents of that hole remain in doubt. It is a fact that nothing of consequence—that can be placed on a table today for examination—has ever been found in digging efforts on Oak Island. The treasure seekers that have scourged that island have looked deep within their earthen pits and found little of value. How much intellectual faith should we put in the verbal accounts of lusty-eyed treasure hunters, or the findings of local labor that relied on digging efforts as a source of income? Little, I think. In their heart-of-hearts, what do they hope to find? Throughout Oak Island's history (and pre-history) there has been opportunity for chicanery, such as deceptive reports and planted evidence. O'Connor offers this connection to Freemasons:

> [Researcher Joe Nickell] points out that many of the early searchers [seven names listed, including 'F.D.R.']... were committed Freemasons, as are a few current theorists about Oak Island. He suggests that some of them, inspired by their Masonic belief that the lost treasures of the Knights Templar (said to include the Holy Grail) were spirited away to some secret vault in the early sixteenth century, seized upon the mysterious [Oak Island] Money Pit as a possible or even probable answer to the whereabouts of those treasures.

Freemasons help to define and perpetuate the Oak Island mystery to this day.

I am inclined to doubt the presence of treasure on the island. Admittedly, this is not a bold position for me to take because only a miracle can prove me wrong. Instead, I entertain the notion that the now-lost markers that initiated the boy's quest were intended to point treasure seekers in a direction other than toward the nine-layered fiery depths of the Earth. But if not down, where? The mathematical elegance and physical permanence of the Oak Island Tree of Life suggested to me that it is a starting point, rather than a destination, for such an investigation. Fred Nolan also seemed to think that the cross would help unlock the mystery. He said, "I have undisputed proof that the Money Pit is a decoy. The proof is over on my property and it's conclusive. It makes the Money Pit a small project in comparison to what I've found." He thought that the treasure lied beneath it. I disagree. "Then he [Nolan] showed me [author William Crooker] a photograph of an artifact that he believes is associated with the cross. It is a lock with a cross-shaped keyhole. When the key is turned, the face opens and another smaller keyhole appears."[3] Let's turn the first key and discover what is hidden beneath the cross.

*****

> And the LORD God said, Behold, the man is become as one of us, to know good and evil: and now, lest he put forth his hand, and take also of the tree of life, and eat, and live for ever. Therefore the LORD God sent him forth from the garden of Eden, to till the ground from whence he was taken. So he drove out the man; and he placed at the east of the garden of Eden Cherubims, and a flaming sword which turned every way, to keep the way of the tree of life.[4]
>   - *Genesis* **3:22**-24

In the Hebrew mystical and philosophical system called the Qabalah, ten points, each called a Sephiroth, create the Tree of Life shape. Three of these points are along the left column, called a pillar by Freemasons; four are along the center column; and three are along the right column. When these points are connected in a particular way, 22 "paths" are created, one for each letter in the Hebrew alphabet.[5] Add the ten Sephiroth to the 22 paths and you get 32 distinct elements.[6] In the Qabalah, each of these 32 elements represents an aspect of personal and spiritual development, with certain aspects of the Deity represented.[7] The 32 degrees, each with its own lesson and initiation, that must be completed before reaching the 33rd degree of Scottish Rite Freemasonry are speculated by some outsiders to derive from the Qabalah Tree of Life. An eleventh Sephiroth is included by some, which I call the Knowledge point (rather than its Hebrew equivalent, transliterated as Da'ath). With this eleventh point, we have 22 + 11 = 33 distinct elements.

---

[3] Crooker, William S. (2014) *Oak Island Gold*. Nimbus. Kindle Ed.

[4] http://www.kingjamesbibleonline.org/Genesis-Chapter-3/

[5] Parfitt, Will. (1999) *The Elements of The Qabalah*. Barnes & Noble, p. 1.

[6] Parfitt, Will. (1999) *The Elements of The Qabalah*. Barnes & Noble, p. 79.

[7] I no doubt have butchered the description of the Qabalah, but its purpose and meaning are not my point here. If you are looking for a more thorough and accurate understanding of the philosophy of the Qabalah start with the Material Girl: http://www.madonna.com/.

For our purpose here, I am setting religious interpretations aside and focusing on the geometric shape on Oak Island. I call it a Tree of Life (TOL) because its stones can be seen to create that shape and because I need a term that the reader can follow. But, I am not endorsing at this time a conclusion that the creators of the stone formation did indeed mean for it to resemble a Qabalah Tree of Life. I'll let the evidence guide me to a conclusion.

The TOL on Oak Island, as described by Amundsen, is 1152 feet long and 720 feet wide. Its width is broken into two halves by the center column of the tree; each half is 360 feet long and perpendicular to the center column. The center column is divided into six segments, two that are 282 feet long and four that are 147 feet long. These dimensions equate to whole numbers only when measured in the English unit of feet, suggesting that the TOL's origin is not, say, ancient alien. I assign to each point (Sephiroth) a number from one to ten using the convention of the Qabalah.[8] I include a circle centered at point [6] with a diameter of 720 feet. I added this circle because the half-width of 360 feet suggested to me a circle of 360 degrees, and point [6] is the center of the shape. This decision proved fortuitous, as will be shown. I also annotated the location of the buried stone on Oak Island, and the so-called Knowledge point, an important point on the Tree of Life, but at which no stone was found (if its location was ever searched). Figure 2 depicts this shape with its length and angular measurements. The black points are Nolan's cross. Amundsen discovered stones at points [7] and [10], but was not permitted to search Nolan's land, on which points [5] and [8] might be buried. Point [4] is in a swamp, possibly man-made, and is central to Amundsen's theory, but not my own. Each of the numbered points will be referred to often in this book; **bookmark this illustration**, or use the visual aid that I put on the last page of the book (turn there now and check it out). I will refer to specific points using this notation: point [#], e.g., point [1]. I will also refer to lines, called "paths," connecting two points like this: path [2]-[3] is the line connecting points [2] and [3]. Note that the length and width dimensions are both divisible by 144 (12 squared), which gives this overall shape an 8-by-5 size ratio (1152 = 8x144; 720 = 5x144). These details are important.

Angular measurements can be made between paths, e.g., path [10]-[9] and path [10]-[8] differ by exactly 40 degrees. These distances and angles will

---

[8] Parfitt, Will. (1999) *The Elements of The Qabalah*. Barnes & Noble, p. 1.

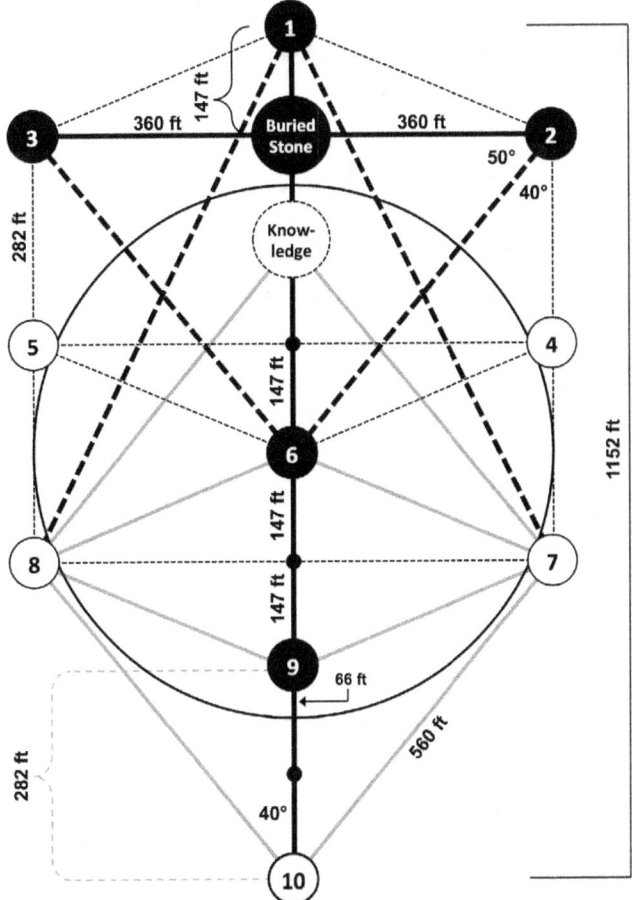

Figure 2: Oak Island Tree of Life (TOL) dimensions

be important as we use this template to examine structures that seem to have been built to this TOL standard. To do so, I will use this TOL template exactly as is, not changing a single length or angle. Rarely, I will use enlarged versions of the template, wherein an increase in one length is matched by a proportional increase in all other lengths, thus preserving the angles and length ratios of the shape. Making the shape wider, for example, without a similar increase in length would distort the shape and send us down the path of finding patterns that are not there. For this book, the theory that I will test uses one shape and only one shape.

Figure 2 depicts a Tree of Life using my own rendering. Its form is consistent with the convention of the Qabalah, but it is not identical. My reasons are not arbitrary. The reader is encouraged to notice four symbolic elements in my rendering (depicted on the first page of Part I). The first element is the Masonic Compass and Square; its lines are thick and dashed. The Compass is formed by connecting points [7]-[1]-[8]. The Square is formed by connecting points [2]-[6]-[3]. The interior angle of this Square is 80 degrees, so it is the visual *symbol* of a square, but not an actual square, which has an interior right angle (90 degrees). Its basic symbolic meaning in Freemasonry is described here:

> The Square is a right angle, formed by two right lines. It is adapted only to a plane surface, and belongs only to geometry, earth-measurement, that trigonometry which deals only with planes, and with the earth, which the ancients supposed to be a plane. The Compass describes circles, and deals with spherical trigonometry, the science of the spheres and heavens. The former, therefore, is an emblem of what concerns the earth and the body; the latter of what concerns the heavens and the soul.[9]

Caution: "The symbols and ceremonies of Masonry have more than one meaning. They rather conceal than disclose the Truth. They hint it only, at least; and their varied meanings are only to be discovered by reflection and study."[10] The second element is two pyramids with their bases touching, one pointing up and the other down. The bases of the pyramids are formed by connecting points [6]-[7]-[9]-[8]. The Knowledge point is the apex of the upward pyramid, and point [10] is the apex of the downward pyramid. As above, so below. "In [some old book] we find the first solid figure, the universal symbol of immortality, the pyramid."[11] The Knowledge point marks the center of the Compass/Square and the summit of the upward pyramid. The third element is the central axis, which is formed by connecting points [1]-[6]-[9]-[10]; a straight connection from top to bottom. This axis is an important feature in the construction of our treasure map, and will prove symbolically vital to deciphering that map. The fourth element is the circle, centered at point [6], bracketed by the left and right pillars. Consider this odd passage that ends the lesson for the Master Mason (Third Degree) in the Freemason text *Morals and Dogma*:

> To the Circle inclosing the central point, and itself traced between two parallel lines, a figure purely Kabalistic, these persons have added the superimposed Bible [cross?], and even reared on that the ladder with

---

[9] Pike, Albert. (1871) *Morals and Dogma*.

[10] Pike, Albert. (1871) *Morals and Dogma*.

[11] Pike, Albert. (1871) *Morals and Dogma*.

three or nine rounds, and then given a vapid interpretation of the whole,
so profoundly absurd as actually to excite admiration.

Masonic literature is filled with odd statements like this, coded language.
Throughout this book I will serve as your guide through this literature,
providing only relevant quotes and highlighting passages that will prove
important to our task ahead. I will give the broader quote so that the reader
may view the context that surrounds the highlighted text. I will introduce the
reader to these texts and their authors later.

The Path

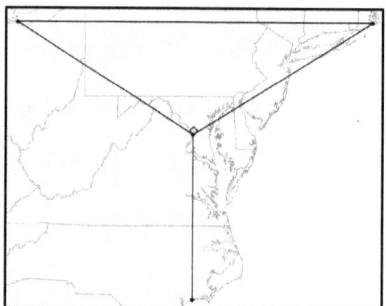

We will now assemble piece-by-piece the first symbol hidden on the American landscape, a chalice, depicted above. With our geometric template (the Tree of Life) in hand, how might we use it to create this map? A quick Internet search will reveal to you many persons attempting to find "alignments" between pyramids, buildings, monuments, streets, cities, etc. They do so looking for evidence of a master plan behind the construction and placement of these things. They're going about it wrong.

To perform these measurements folks seem to turn to the easiest tool available: Google Earth and its "ruler" tool. I'll endorse Google Earth here as a wonderful program for examining shapes and distances on the three-dimensional globe, but it has a shortfall that seems to have gone unnoticed.

Navigators before our recent technological era lacked the ability to accurately measure the distance traveled between points beyond the horizon because they lacked the ability to accurately determine longitude, particularly while in motion on the open ocean. They also lacked the mathematical understanding needed to accurately draw shortest-distance paths (called geodesic paths) on a three-dimensional ellipsoid surface (Earth). The mathematics needed for an accurate geodesic calculation matured in the mid-nineteenth century (lookup Bernhard Reimann). So, they needed a means of plotting a course from one point to another that could be followed using the tools available to them, which were celestial navigation (determining course and latitude by the position of the sun and the stars), a compass (magnetic north), and two-dimensional *hand-calculated* geometry.

In 1569, Gerard Mercator created a map projection of the world using a new means of projecting the three-dimensional surface of the Earth onto a two-dimensional map: the Mercator projection. You have seen this world map all of your life. It notoriously distorts the size of landmasses near the poles, so Greenland looks larger than the United States, and Antarctica looks larger than Africa. In *Rhumb Lines and Map Wars*, Mark Monmonier details the history of the Mercator projection and the political battles that surround it. Namely, some feel that its visual distortions, which were done for practical navigational purposes, contribute to an unfair social hierarchy, because the lands of northern (read white and affluent) nations are visually aggrandized while the lands of equatorial (read non-white and third world) nations are visually diminished by comparison. This is an aside, but for me it was a new and interesting one.

For our purposes, forgive the Mercator projection its distortions. They have a purpose that fueled the age of exploration. Note that all of the vertical (longitude) and horizontal (latitude) lines on the Mercator projection are straight from end-to-end and are perfectly aligned up-down and side-to-side (see Figure 3). If you take a straight edge, such as a ruler, and draw a straight line—in any direction—on a Mercator projection, then the angle between that line and north is the same across the entire length of your line. In other words, if you had a compass and the North Star, you could follow the path that you drew by maintaining a single bearing relative to north.

When looking at your path on a Mercator projection it appears to be a straight line, but in reality, on the curved surface of the Earth, you are traveling in an arc (see Figure 3). It is not the shortest path. But, in the 17th century you took what you could get. The line that you drew on your

Mercator projection is called a rhumb line (or loxodrome). Here is a definition of a rhumb line that I pulled from the Internet (mathworks.com):

> A rhumb line is a curve that crosses each meridian [north-south line] at the same angle. This curve is also referred to as a loxodrome (from the Greek loxos, slanted, and drome, path). Although a great circle is a shortest path, it is difficult to navigate because your bearing (or azimuth) continuously changes as you proceed. Following a rhumb line covers more distance than following a geodesic, but it is easier to navigate.

Back to Google Earth. If you turn on the "ruler" feature on Google Earth, or any of the tools for creating shapes and paths, they create great circle (or geodesic) lines. I could not find any means of plotting a rhumb line using Google Earth. Today, with the use of Global Positioning System (GPS) navigation and portable computers, we can follow shortest distance (geodesic) paths easily. Rhumb lines are essentially obsolete. But, in this book we are seeking to uncover a plan set into motion long before GPS. The plan would have been created using the state-of-the-art navigation of the time: rhumb lines. But, the researchers that I've observed on the Internet, in books, and

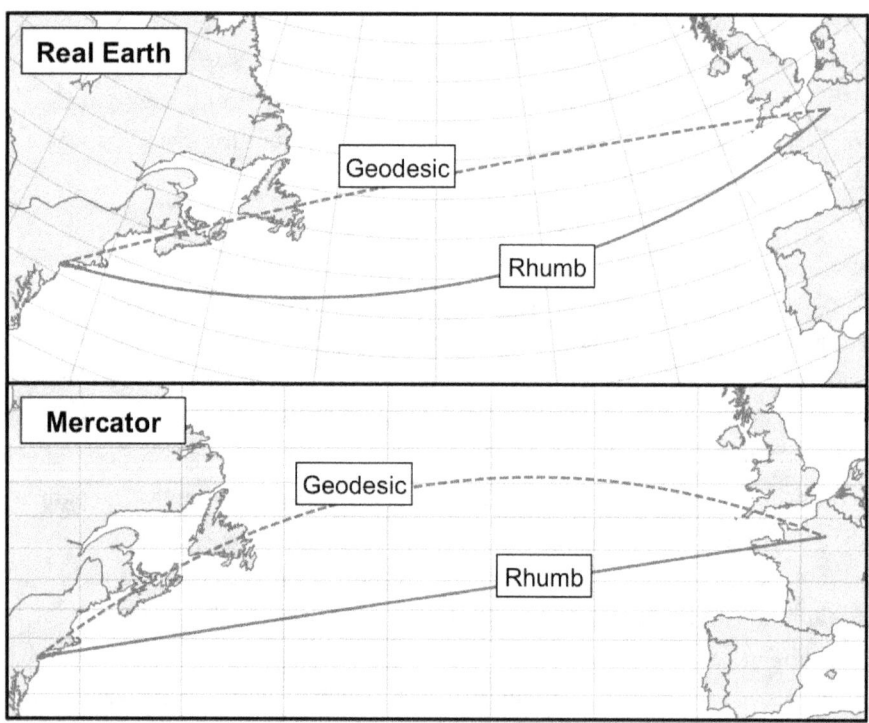

Figure 3: Rhumb and geodesic lines. Rhumb line keeps constant bearing to north.

on television all use Google Earth. As such, they are plotting geodesic lines.

How much of a difference does this make? Let us consider a path from Oak Island to the center of Washington DC's square borders. Using a geodesic line, one would need to travel on a bearing of 243.90 degrees relative to true north (note that all bearings in this book are relative to true north, unless otherwise stated; see Figure 4). The distance along this path is 763.58 miles. Using a rhumb line, one would need to travel on an azimuth of 239.50 degrees for 764.28 miles. The difference in bearing (4.4 degrees) between these two paths is what's most important. If one followed the geodesic bearing and distance but used a rhumb line (constant compass bearing) path then they would end up 61.08 miles northwest of the center of Washington DC. That is not a minor navigational error, unless you are willing to substitute your vacation in the Nation's capital for a Little League game in Chewsville, Maryland (39.64523116,-77.64139794).[12] I have no doubt it's a

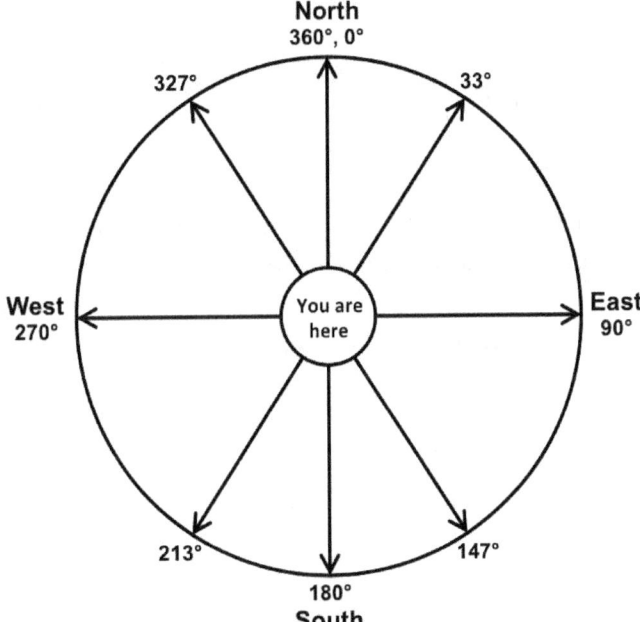

Figure 4: Geographic bearings measured relative to true north.

[12] I will use this format to present geo-coordinates (latitude, longitude). Just type these numbers, separated by a comma, into the search field of your favorite mapping program and you should be taken to these coordinates.

fine place. Over short distances, measured in dozens to a few hundred feet, the difference between these two paths is unnoticeable, but it is quite sizable, as shown above, over longer distances.

The numbers shown above are the coordinates of a point on the Earth (latitude, longitude). For those unfamiliar with these terms, latitude is the number that tells us how far north-south we are, with the equator having a latitude of zero, the north pole 90 degrees, and the south pole -90 degrees. Longitude reflects the angle around the Earth from the Prime Meridian, which is a line running from the south pole to the north pole, and passing through a spot near London. If you imagine yourself in outer space looking down on England, then the Prime Meridian represents a longitude of zero degrees. Anything to the right (toward the Middle East and Asia) has a positive longitude, and anything to the left (toward America) has a negative longitude. Look again at the coordinate above for Chewsville. It has a positive latitude because Maryland is north of the equator, and a negative longitude because it is west of England. Sometimes a coordinate will be represented using this format: Degrees-Minutes-Seconds. In this format, there are 360 degrees in a circle. You already knew that. There are 60 minutes in a degree, and there are 60 seconds in a minute. So, the minutes and seconds represent the fraction of a degree. I mention this because some of our clues are hidden in these numbers. For example, the longitude for the U.S. Capital Building can be written as 77°00'33.0" W (W means west of the Prime Meridian, or a negative number). Do you see the 33 in there? This is not a coincidence. It will come up again.

I began my research where others began, using Google Earth and geodesic lines. I did not find a consistent pattern, though, until I began using the navigational tools of the time period that I was investigating. Henceforth, be it known that all lines in this book will be rhumb lines. But, how does one calculate a rhumb line? Carefully, of course.

*****

Skip to the next chapter, unless you are interested in the coding aspect of this investigation. In the appendix, I give the geographic coordinates used in my analysis and I provide the code for creating the curves that constitute the bulk of my analysis. But, to get you started, here is the code in Mathematica v10 that I used to perform the calculations mentioned above. Before you ask,

ITRF00 is the short name of an ellipsoid that approximates the shape of the Earth. It stands for International Terrestrial Reference Frame (2000). People don't calculate coordinates, distances, and such on the actual Earth; they calculate them on a mathematical model of the Earth. ITRF00 is such a model.

In the Mathematica programming language, characters inside the (* *) enclosure are comments for the programmer's benefit and are ignored during execution of the program. A semi-colon at the end of a line suppresses the output display of the line. I don't need the program to repeat back to me the constants that I am giving it, just the results of the calculations.

```
ftpm = 3.280839895; (* feet per meter *)
mpmi = 5280/ftpm;   (* meters per mile *)
(* Oak Island coordinate: point [10] from Amundsen book *)
oakisland = GeoPosition[{FromDMS[{44, 30, 46.5864}],
    -FromDMS[{64, 17, 41.5134}]},"ITRF00"];
(* Coordinate for center of DC diamond *)
DCcenter = GeoPosition[{38.892818,-77.041046},"ITRF00"];
(* Distance from Oak Island to DC center along geodesic *)
GeoDisplacement[oakisland,DCcenter,"Geodesic"][[1]][[1]]/mpmi
(* Azimuth from Oak Island to DC center along geodesic *)
GeoDisplacement[oakisland, DCcenter, "Geodesic"][[1]][[2]]
(* Distance from Oak Island to DC center along rhumb *)
GeoDisplacement[oakisland, DCcenter, "Rhumb"][[1]][[1]]/mpmi
(* Azimuth from Oak Island to DC center along rhumb *)
GeoDisplacement[oakisland, DCcenter, "Rhumb"][[1]][[2]]
(* Distance from DC to erroneous point described above *)
GeoDisplacement[DCcenter,GeoDestination[oakisland,
        GeoDisplacement[{
            GeoDisplacement[oakisland,DCcenter,
                "Geodesic"][[1]][[1]], (* distance *)
            GeoDisplacement[oakisland,DCcenter,
                "Geodesic"][[1]][[2]]}, (* azimuth *)
            "Rhumb"]],"Geodesic"][[1]][[1]]/mpmi
```

The Unfinished Temple

Now that we are armed with the Oak Island Tree of Life (TOL) template, a starting point (Oak Island), and a means for navigating to other destinations (rhumb line) we can begin our quest for the next location in the mystery. One way that we could search for the next location is to take our TOL template and spend countless hours plopping it randomly over places with obvious Masonic influences, like Washington DC. Admittedly, I have done this. But, it is a big world and we need a more scientific approach. Also, when I began this investigation at Oak Island, I did not suspect in the slightest that Freemasons had anything to do with it. We need to hypothesize how the Oak Island TOL might have been intended to vector an explorer and then we need to stick to that methodology. If the approach does not work, then it must be discarded as a theory. We cannot choose one approach at one location and another approach elsewhere as we attempt to find *any* means to get to places of biased interest, e.g., Washington DC. To start, I chose two means of getting from point A to point B. First, we could follow the path lines created by connecting any two Sephiroth (points) on the TOL template. This approach is straightforward. Perhaps the stones on Oak Island were positioned with the intent to point treasure seekers in a direction. The center column of the Tree of Life, which in my rendering contains a Masonic Compass and Square, seems of particular importance. In the Scottish Rite

Freemasonry text *Morals and Dogma*, Albert Pike made the following note in a
paragraph about the Tree of Life:

> [W]henever you depart from the centre of the Square and the Compass
> you will no longer be able to work with success.

Second, we could follow the azimuth of sunrise and sunset on the solstices
and equinoxes, as seen at the location of our TOL. Why? There are two
solstices each year: one to mark the beginning of summer (usually 21 June)
and one to mark the beginning of winter (usually 21 December). The Earth is
tilted on its axis relative to its orbit around the Sun. As such, during summer
the Earth leans toward the Sun, and during winter it leans away from the Sun.
This leaning toward and away from its heat source (sun) is the cause of the
seasons. The summer solstice offers the longest period of sunlight every year,
rising early and setting late. The winter solstice offers the shortest period of
sunlight, rising late and setting early. One can symbolically view the winter
solstice as a moment of rebirth, since all days after it will be longer than the
day before (like an infant growing each day), until the summer solstice, which
symbolizes the onset of decay (maturity). These extremes are more dramatic
the further that one is from the equator, with northern latitudes experiencing
longer days in the summer than those at the equator. The equinoxes mark the
beginning of spring and autumn (usually around 20 March and 22 September)
and offer equal amounts of light and darkness (about 12 hours between
sunrise and sunset). They can be viewed symbolically to represent balance
and harmony. The solstices and equinoxes are used by Freemasons as
symbols and have been important to peoples of all cultures throughout
human history. At some level, we all worship the sun god.

Starting with the first approach, using the Oak Island Tree of Life paths
as pointers, we immediately encounter a problem. Amundsen explained it
well (he says cone where I say stone because the stones had a cone shape):
"...we learn that the top cone [point 1 of the TOL] had been removed by
[Fred] Nolan a few years earlier (they measured at the hole in the ground), so
it is impossible to know exactly where the tip of the cone was." The treasure
hunters' dig-first, think-second approach has trampled our clues. How can
we determine the bearing of the center column of the TOL if we don't know
exactly where the tip of the column is located? Fortunately, three other
points remain. There is another problem, even if the top cone had not been
removed. The stones are large and rounded at the top, so determining the
location of their center is subjective. Last, the most accurate geolocation

information for the stones (cones), as far as I can tell, comes from Petter Amundsen's GPS readings. GPS positions contain errors that are exacerbated by bad weather (interference of the satellite signal), as Amundsen's were: "as a relentless rainstorm bid us welcome to Oak Island." His GPS device gathered sensitive timing signals from satellites more than 12,000 miles away—through a rainstorm.

Why does all of this matter? The location and orientation of the Oak Island TOL stones is the only part of my investigation that suffers from a *very slight* inaccuracy, as you will soon see. Unfortunately, that error is at the start of our investigation and while I'm still trying to earn your trust. So, hang in there with me for one hop. I know how this ends. We will validate the choice that I made here in a surprising and compelling way.

Amundsen provided three GPS coordinates related to the center column of the Oak Island Tree of Life. They are (latitude, longitude):

Point [6] = (44.51373661,-64.29295547)
Point [9] = (44.51333381,-64.29392383)
Point [10] = (44.51294067,-64.29486483)

The bearings between these points are:

[6]-[9]:   239.82913645 degrees
[6]-[10]:   239.77583547 degrees
[9]-[10]:   239.72036678 degrees
Average: 239.7751129 degrees

Using the average bearing, we can conclude that the center column of the Oak Island TOL bears 239.78 degrees, or 59.78 degrees in the opposite direction. The sun rises on Oak Island on the summer solstice at 55.1 degrees—nearly a five-degree difference, so no reasonable amount of measuring error can suggest that the Oak Island TOL is oriented with the solstices. Further, I found no meaningful alignment with the solstices along any of the TOL paths at Oak Island. It might point to something else.

The northeastern path (59.78 degrees) points toward the North Atlantic—nothing that way. The southwestern path (239.78 degrees) points through Newport, RI and Washington DC (along a rhumb line). This rhumb line, to my eye, passes somewhat vaguely through central Washington DC. It doesn't intersect the White House, the Capital Building, the Scottish Rite building north of the White House, the Pentagon, or any monument that I could see. Nor does it align with the diagonal streets in the center of the city.

But, it is a direct hit on the diamond shape of Washington, DC.[13] What about Newport?

Any person familiar with the Freemason or Knights Templar genre of conspiracy theories has heard of the Newport Tower. Debates about its origins, age, and meaning fill books, blogs, and hot air. The speculated construction dates of the tower vary widely, with some even suggesting that it was built more than 500 years ago, destroyed, and then rebuilt. Its apparent reference in the will of Benedict Arnold, the first colonial governor of Rhode Island (not his descendent, the notorious British spy), places its origin before 1677. Newport, the town, was founded in 1639. A somewhat newer theory, offered by Danish researcher Jorgen Siemonsen, looking into the question of Viking origin, concludes that Freemasons built the tower in the 1750s, according to an article in the Boston Globe.[14]

Circumstantial evidence, Siemonsen said, points toward the fledgling Freemason movement in Rhode Island and a well-connected, English-trained architect who found work among the rich and famous of Colonial Newport.

That architect, Peter Harrison, laid out an octagon summer house in the mid-1700s for Abraham Redwood, a wealthy Newport merchant, Siemonsen said. That geometric form, closely associated with the Freemasons, is mimicked in the eight pillars of the tower, a little more than a block away, that Siemonsen speculated Harrison also designed....

Carbon-14 testing of the tower's mortar points to 1740 to 1810 as the most likely period of construction, Siemonsen said. That result, coupled with Harrison's exposure to octagon design in England and the founding of a Masonic lodge in Newport in 1749, help Siemonsen buoy his theory.

The azimuth from the bottom stone on the Oak Island TOL (point [10]) to the Newport Tower, along a rhumb line, is 239.54 degrees. If Amundsen's TOL azimuth of 239.78 degrees were adjusted by less than a quarter of a degree then it would point directly at the Newport Tower. Such an error would result if the GPS coordinates of the TOL end points (points [1] and [10]) were off by a combined total of 4.8 feet,[15] which is a fraction of a

---

[13] At my adjusted bearing, it passes through the original campus of The George Washington University.

[14] MacQuarrie, Brian. "Tower's past a Present Puzzle." *Boston.com.* 20 Sept. 2010.

[15] 1152 ft length * tan[0.24 degrees] = 4.83 ft

Figure 5: Newport Tower

percent of the TOL's total length. Given the three sources of GPS error mentioned above (weather, rounded top, and missing stone [1]), plus the stated potential error of GPS generally, a 4.8 foot error is well within reason. Note this statement from gps.gov, which only promises better than an 11.5 foot accuracy for GPS: "Real-world data from the FAA show that their high-quality GPS SPS receivers provide better than 3.5 meter [11.5 feet] horizontal accuracy."

If you will forgive this 0.24 degree inaccuracy and consider that the Oak Island TOL points along a rhumb line to the Newport Tower, then we are in business. The Newport Tower is not our final destination. As I will soon demonstrate, it is the cornerstone of a larger landscape.

The Newport Tower is perhaps most notable for its solstice alignments. Academic studies of the tower reveal that its oddly placed windows form alignments so that sunlight on the solstices shines through them and illuminates structures inside the tower. Frenzied masses of people gather at the tower on solstice days to bear witness to sunlight shining through those tower windows. And by "frenzied" I mean "latte-sipping" and possibly "toga wearing." I've never been. So, let us begin with a solstice azimuth.

At the Newport Tower, the sun sets on the winter solstice at an azimuth of 238.756 degrees, according to Mathematica v10. Here is the code.

```
nptower = GeoPosition[{41.485818, -71.309856}, "ITRF00"];
winsoldate = DateObject[{2014, 12, 21, 0, 0}];
time = Sunset[{Latitude[nptower], Longitude[nptower]},
          winsoldate];
FromDMS[StarData["Sun",
    EntityProperty["Star","Azimuth",
        {"Date" -> time, "Location" -> nptower}]]]
```

A rhumb line from the Newport Tower along this solstice azimuth runs slightly south of the rhumb line on the Oak Island TOL azimuth (239.54 degrees). It passes vaguely through southeastern Washington DC. I did not observe it pass through any DC monuments or buildings of note, or demonstrate alignment with any streets. It seems to pass through the third mile marker from the eastern corner of DC on the southeastern border, near Cedar Hill and Washington National cemeteries. The borders of DC were originally formed using stone mile markers along each side, placed a mile apart for 10 miles. Some of them still remain. Plug this coordinate (38.933699, -76.961347) into your favorite mapping program and observe the stubby cement object surrounded by a short black fence in the corner of someone's yard. Google Street View provides a good look. This alignment of the rhumb line and a mile marker is probably a coincidence.

More interestingly, the rhumb line from the Newport Tower on the winter solstice sunset azimuth passes through the grounds of the George Washington Masonic National Memorial, which is located in Alexandria, Virginia, just outside Washington DC.

Buckle up.

The Lighthouse at Alexandria

The George Washington Masonic National Memorial (hereafter GW MM) is an impressive 333-foot tall stone building, started in 1922, which sits atop Shuter's Hill, a prime piece of real estate overlooking Alexandria, VA and Washington DC beyond. When Washington DC was first created some of what is now Alexandria sat within its diamond-shaped borders (DC was a 10-by-10 mile square rotated 45 degrees). This land was given back (retroceded) to the state of Virginia in 1846, giving the modern borders of DC a bit of an imperfect and unfinished look. The GW MM sits immediately outside that original DC boundary. The official website for the Memorial offers this note on the importance of this particular location:

> The site was selected because it followed the ancient tradition for the location of temples on hilltops or mountains. It was also located on land with which General Washington was familiar; it was the very spot once proposed by Thomas Jefferson as the ideal site for the nation's Capitol.[16]

Featured prominently in Old Town Alexandria, within the original DC border, is King Street. It runs from the Potomac river at a bearing of 279.25 degrees for nearly 1.5 miles before it bends toward the northwest at the original southwest DC border, and at the entrance to the GW MM grounds.

---

[16] www.gwmemorial.org/history.php

If King St continued straight, rather than curving northward, it would pass through the GW MM, as the monument grounds are also aligned on a 279.25 degree axis (99.25 degrees in the other direction) and are centered perfectly with Old Town King St.

Starting at the King St bend, one approaches the GW MM by walking up Shuter's Hill along concrete paths built into the grounds. These paths start at a sidewalk along the entry road and then separate into two straight and parallel paths that join again at a concrete platform featuring a bust of George Washington. They separate again into winding paths (mirror reflections of each other about the 279.25 degree axis) that are joined by another crossing path, and later converge at a platform that connects to steps. One then crosses a road on the grounds and is faced by a large set of steps at the base of the memorial. Atop these steps one is level with the entrance floor of the memorial and is standing in front of the large pillars that mark the entrance to the memorial. The front door is about 20 feet beyond the pillars.

A solid fence surrounds the building, except on its eastern-facing front. It's a short wall, really, but I do not want to confuse you with the walls of the

Figure 6: George Washington Masonic National Memorial and Alexandria War Dead Monument

monument building itself, so I'll call it a fence. The dimensions of the fence, according to my Google Earth measurements, seem to be 225 by 256 feet in length. These dimensions are the squares of 15 and 16. Freemasons are geometry nerds. Atop the building is a three-tiered tower designed to look like the lighthouse at Alexandria (Egypt, not Virginia), which is capped by a pyramid with a beacon on top. The building is rectangular in shape, except for the western (back) side, which is semi-circular and encloses an auditorium.

Placing the Oak Island TOL over this landscape reveals a number of dimensional similarities (see Figure 7). I put point [1], the top of the TOL, at the center of the western (circular) wall. By doing so, the location on the TOL where the buried "face" stone was found on Oak Island sits directly beneath the GW MM tower. Is something buried in the hill beneath it? Point [9] sits near the start of the walkways at the bottom of the hill. A line between points [7] and [8] (path [7]-[8]) crosses the next platform, where the sidewalks change from straight to curvy. In Figure 6, this point is visible, as it sits at the bust of George Washington, beneath which is this quote: "Let prejudices and local interests yield to reason. Let us look to our national character and to things beyond the present period." Point [6] sits at the next crossing path. A line between points [4] and [5] crosses the next platform, at the base of the steps before the road. The midpoint between the tower (buried stone) and the path [4]-[5] intersection sits at the top of the steps to the memorial building.

Point [10] sits at the bend in King St, where King St shifts from its 279.25 degree azimuth toward the north. This point is due north of a nearby monument (114 feet away), the Alexandria War Dead Monument,[17] which was created from a pillar intended for the GW MM, but that was broken during construction.[18]

---

[17] The plaque on the monument's side reads in part: "Erected in memory of Alexandria War Dead... November 11, 1940."

[18] "Each column was 18 feet (5.5 m) high and 4.5 feet (1.4 m) in diameter, and arrived at Alexandria's Union Station by train from Redstone, New Hampshire. One columnar section was damaged, and given to the Ladies Auxiliary of the Veterans of Foreign Wars (VFW). The VFW turned it into a memorial to American war dead, and erected it in front of Alexandria's Union Station." http://en.wikipedia.org/wiki/George_Washington_Masonic_National_Memorial, sourced from Brown, Adrian Brown, 1980. History of the George Washington

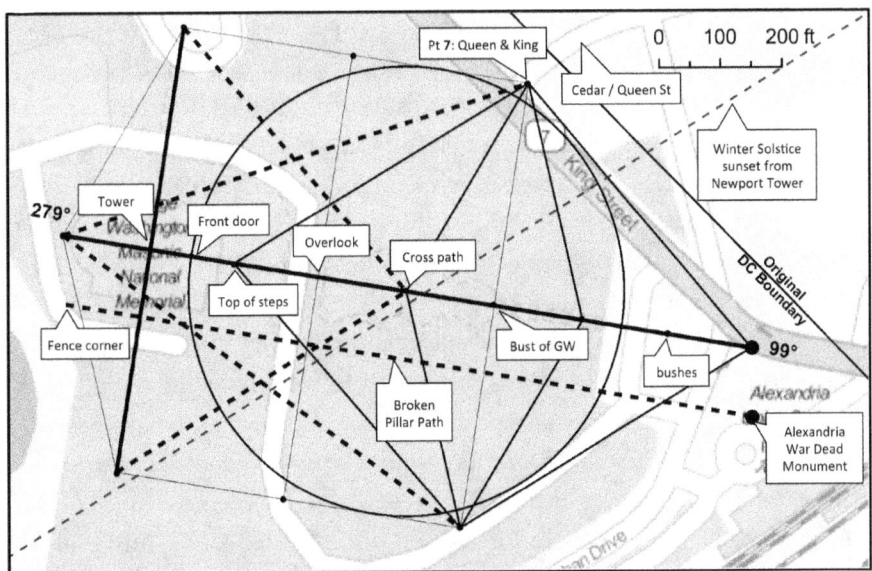

Figure 7: George Washington Masonic National Memorial and its Tree of Life

Every point along the center column of the TOL aligns perfectly with a major feature of the building or its landscape. But what else? In Qabalah symbolism point [9] is called Queen and point [6] is called King. Points [9] and [6] each form a Qabalah path with point [7]. In other words, point [7] can be considered to be an intersection of the King and Queen points on the TOL. On the GW MM TOL that I am describing here, point [7] sits at the intersection of King St (on its northwesterly route) and Queen St. Now, to be fair, Queen St, as it is called in Old Town stops at the railroad tracks a few hundred feet from the GW MM grounds. It is continued under the name Cedar St, which is also important. But, if the Queen St name had been continued across the tracks, as King St was, they would intersect exactly at point [7]. King St is Virginia Route 7.

Recall that the length of the TOL template is 1152 feet. The Alexandria War Dead Monument across the street from the GW MM, and due south of point [10], aligns perfectly with the southern fence of the memorial and is 1152 feet from the southwest corner of the fence. I annotate this line on Figure 7 as the "Broken Pillar Path." The War Dead Monument faces a bearing of 345 degrees (down Russell Rd), which differs from the 279 degree

Masonic National Memorial. Alexandria, VA: The George Washington Masonic National Memorial Association.

orientation of the GW MM by 66 degrees. Remember the number 66 (2x33), as it will recur often and prove central to this overall Masonic plan.

What about that Newport Tower solstice path that led us here? It passes almost exactly through the path created by points [6] and [3] (path [6]-[3]). It misses them by a few feet, which is two ten-thousandth of a degree off from a direct hit. At that distance (356 miles), this is effectively an exact hit on point [6]. Path [6]-[3] is 40.0 degrees off the main axis of the TOL, so on the GW MM TOL it has an azimuth of 239.25 degrees (279.25 - 40.0). Recall that the Newport Tower winter solstice sunset azimuth was 238.76 degrees, so these two paths differ by a half-degree. That's not bad for folks without satellite imagery and GPS, given the distance involved.

In *Morals and Dogma* (1871), Albert Pike, Grand Commander of the Ancient and Accepted Scottish Rite of Freemasonry, Supreme Council of the Thirty-Third Degree, Southern Jurisdiction of the United States, provided teachings as lengthy as his title on each of the 32 initiation degrees of that Order. I will reference this book often, as it seems an authoritative source on Scottish Rite Freemasonry, as published officially by Freemasons. Pike writes [emphasis added]: "...Therefore it must be re-vivified, and made to be born again from its ashes, which you will effect by virtue of the vegetation of the *Tree of Life, represented to us by the branch of acacia.*" This is one of the few mentions of the Tree of Life in this lengthy book. I equate acacia in this quote with cedar, as they are two evergreens that have interchangeable symbolic meaning in Masonry. Cedar and Acacia are often found in the names of Masonic cemeteries, since these evergreens symbolize eternal life. Also, as noted by Freemasons, cedar was used in the construction of the Temple of Solomon in Jerusalem and in the Ark of the Covenant, helping create non-degradable structures. Perhaps more importantly to symbolic Freemasonry, in Egyptian myth it was acacia (cedar) that took root around the body of the murdered Osiris, the sun god, at the time of his resurrection. As such, cedar symbolizes strong roots, a lasting foundation, and immortality.

Meanwhile, back in Alexandria, Virginia, the reader should note that point [7] on the GW MM TOL rests on beginning of Cedar St. When I noticed Cedar St. at the GW MM, given the quote and symbolism above, I added cedar to my theory as a potential marker for where a Tree of Life might be found.

I consider these similarities between the GW MM grounds and the Oak Island TOL template to be difficult to dismiss as coincidence. They suggest that the GW MM was placed where it is, in the orientation that it is, to conform to the Oak Island TOL shape and to align with the Newport Tower on the winter solstice. So, even if one doubts the correctness of my quarter-degree correction to the calculated orientation of the Oak Island TOL, the presence of TOL dimensions and related symbolism on the GW MM grounds and its alignment with the Newport Tower winter solstice sunset path indicates that Oak Island, the Newport Tower, and the GW MM are part of a single plan. But, don't judge yet; we're just getting started.

The Virgin and the Pillar

I am time, the destroyer of all; I have come to consume the world. Even without your participation [in this battle], all the warriors gathered here will die [eventually]. Therefore arise; conquer your enemies [within you] and enjoy the glory of sovereignty [liberty]. I have already slain all these warriors; you will only be my instrument.[19]

    - *The Bhagavad Gita*

A fair reading of religious history reveals consistent symbolic and ritualistic themes across belief systems, cultures, and time periods. One such theme places an importance on the virgin, or maiden, often represented by the constellation Virgo. Figure 8 is called in Masonic literature "The Beautiful Virgin of the Third Degree," as in the third (or Master) degree of Freemasonry. The artistic representation of this Masonic lesson, which includes the virgin standing over a broken pillar, has several forms, and there is an open debate within the Masonic community as to its proper form and meaning.[20] A Freemason website (seemingly run by Freemasons, not

---

[19] *The Bhagavad Gita* 11:32-33. (1985). (E. Easwaran trans). Nigiri Press.
[20] Brown , Robert Hewitt. (1882) *Stellar Theology and Masonic Astronomy.*

conspiracy theorists) includes the following claim about the broken column depicted in Figure 8:

> The Broken Column is believed to be a fairly recent addition to the symbolism of Freemasonry, and has been attributed to Brother Jeremy L. Cross. Brother Cross is said to have devised the symbol based upon a broken column grave monument dedicated to a Commodore Lawrence, which was erected in the Trinity Churchyard circa 1813. Lawrence perished in a naval battle that same year between the Frigates Chesapeake and Shannon. The illustration of the broken column was reportedly first published in the "True Masonic Chart" by artist Amos Doolittle in 1819. There is however little evidence beyond the word of Brother Cross that the symbol was thus created.[21]

The "Trinity Churchyard" is that of Trinity Church in lower Manhattan, a site that has several alignments suggesting it to be part of a Tree of Life layout, as will be seen later. Pike, in *Morals and Dogma*, offers this comment on our Virgin:

> Blue Masonry [basic Craft Masonry], ignorant of its import, still retains among its emblems one of a woman weeping over a broken column, holding in her hand a branch of acacia, myrtle, or tamarisk, while Time, we are told, stands behind her combing out the ringlets of her hair. We need not repeat the vapid and trivial explanation there given, of this representation of Isis, weeping at Byblos, over the column torn from the palace of the living, that contained the body of Osiris, while Horus, the God of Time, pours ambrosia on her hair.

It does not serve our purpose here to wade into the debate about the origin and meaning of this artistic rendering. Rather, I add it to our discussion because Figure 8 appears to have been created in accordance with the Tree of Life dimensions. I also have seen other Masonic artwork that conforms wonderfully to the Oak Island Tree of Life, such as *Masonic Emblems*[22] published by George Kenning in 1874, and *Light and Truth*, which is available for purchase under that name at bookstores.

I'll limit our discussion here to this particular rendering of the beautiful virgin, her broken pillar, and cedar branch. Placing the TOL template over the picture such that the circle in the TOL, centered at point [6], overlays the

---

[21] http://www.freemasons-freemasonry.com/broken-column.html

[22] http://freemasonry.bcy.ca/art/masonic_emblems1874.jpg

circle in the artwork, the following alignments between this image and the Tree of Life template are observed:

- Point [6] is at the virgin's womb.
- Path [4]-[5] intersects the center column at the virgin's shoulder.
- Path [7]-[8] intersects the center column at the virgin's feet.
- The winged man (Father Time) is standing on path [7]-[8].
- Path [7]-[8] passes through the line where the pillar and its base meet.
- Path [9]-[8] passes through the bottom of the pillar top, which has fallen.
- Path [8]-[Knowledge], path [4]-[5], and path [6]-[3] intersect at the virgin's hand, which is holding a branch of acacia (cedar). (Make a mental note of this intersection.)
- Point [9] is at the base of the three steps.
- Path [6]-[2] intersects path [7]-[1] where Father Time's wing joins his shoulder.
- Path [1]-[7] clips the wings of Father Time. Have fun with this Masonic-sounding excerpt from *Lamia*, a poem about a maiden by John Keats (1820): "Philosophy will clip an Angel's wings, / Conquer all mysteries by rule and line."[23]

Now return to the Tree of Life at the George Washington Masonic National Memorial. Recall that 114 feet south of point [10] of this TOL is the Alexandria War Dead Monument, which is made from a pillar originally intended for the GW MM, but that was donated for the War Dead Monument when the pillar was broken during construction. This monument is 1152 feet (the length of the TOL template) from the southwest corner of the fence surrounding the GW MM. A line from the War Dead Monument to that southwest corner is perfectly aligned with the GW MM southern fence. If "The Beautiful Virgin of the Third Degree" is placed over the GW

---

[23] It seems to me unlikely that Keats has any role in this American plan, given his short life lived in Europe (died at 25), but he may have drawn inspiration from texts that also influenced the Freemasons of his time. For more on Keats and Freemasonry consider starting your research at http://moon-books.net/blogs/moonbooks/nature-mystics-john-keats/, which observes: "One study by Jennifer Wunder has examined his [Keats's] links to Hermeticism and secret societies, such as the Rosicrucian order and Freemasonry, and has found a consistent pattern of hermetic imagery within his poetry." "While there is no clear evidence to suggest that Keats was actually a member of the Rosicrucian Fraternity or the Freemasons, the imagery used by both movements shows up repeatedly in his poetry and his letters, so much so that it is too clear to be passed off as a coincidence."

MM Tree of Life (similar to Figure 8), then the line from the War Dead Monument (broken pillar) to the southwest fence corner follows the edge of the upright broken pillar in the artwork. This alignment suggests that the War Dead Monument was placed deliberately to conform to the Tree of Life and Third Degree artwork. Perhaps the donated pillar was broken intentionally to satisfy this symbolic purpose. We'll return to the virgin and her cedar branch later. Time, eventually, will reveal the secrets that she withholds.

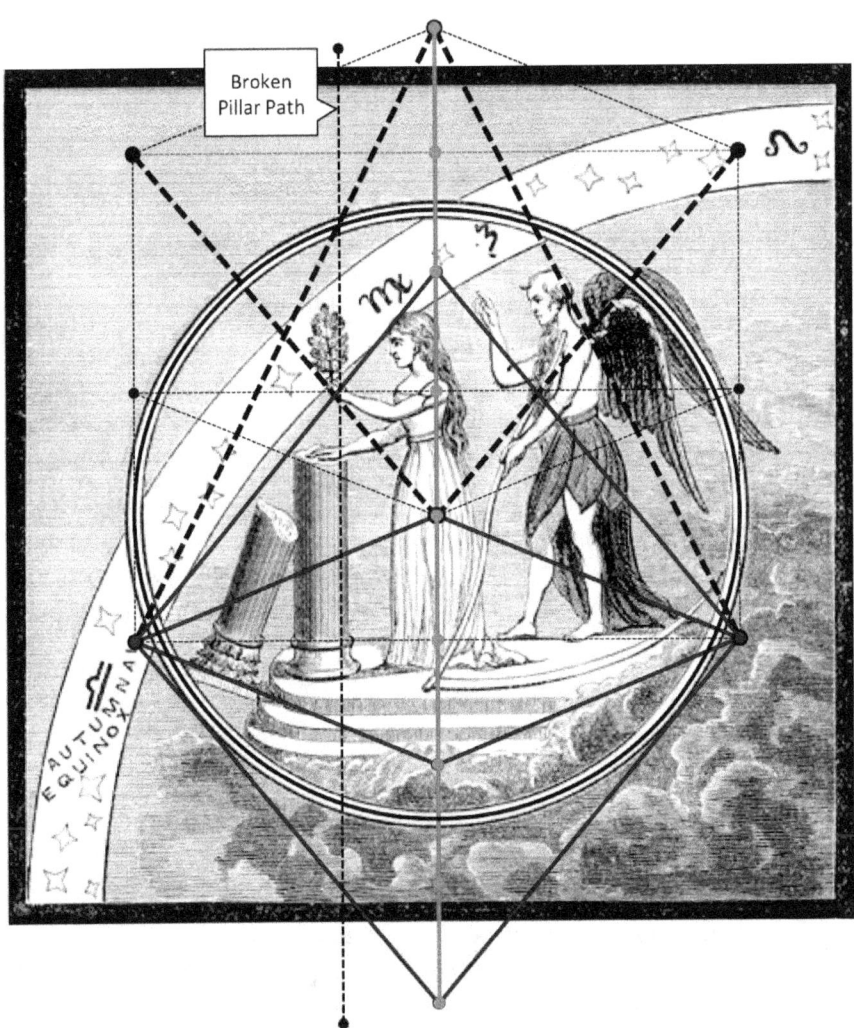

Figure 8: "The Beautiful Virgin of the Third Degree"
with Masonic Tree of Life overlay.

The Veil of Symbols

Before I take you to the next alignment, let us reflect on the implications of the Tree of Life (TOL) alignment with the George Washington Masonic National Memorial (GW MM) grounds. If the GW MM was built to conform to the Oak Island Tree of Life, then either the Freemasons (who openly built and own the GW MM) adopted the Oak Island shape, which allegedly was not discovered until 1981, or they were involved in the creation of the Oak Island TOL before the island became the near-constant residence of treasure hunters in 1795. Further, the fact that the Oak Island TOL points to the Newport Tower, and that the tower points to the GW MM TOL along the winter solstice sunset azimuth, is evidence that the Newport Tower is a Masonic structure, as has been argued, and not a viking (or other) structure, as has been speculated. If the Newport Tower is Masonic, as might be the case, then its construction is odd; why is it not in a more finished condition? Surely, the Freemasons were capable of building something that would better endure a few hundred years.

And why the Tree of Life? While undoubtedly a symbol of the Qabalah, from which Freemasonry openly borrows much of its symbolism, can we conclude that the Tree of Life is also a Masonic symbol? To answer this question I will escort the reader through some Masonic literature. The excerpts below aim to examine the relevance of the Tree of Life, and the

Qabalah generally, within Freemason philosophy, and relate to the creation or deciphering of our map. These passages may be difficult for some readers to digest, as they discuss an Order (Freemasonry) and symbols that are unfamiliar to many. I explain these topics in detail in a later chapter because I aim to limit distractions at this time that will delay the reader's arrival at our first complete map element (only two chapters away).

I find three mentions of the Tree of Life by name in the Scottish Rite publication *Morals and Dogma* (1871): 1) "Analogy gives the Sage all the forces of Nature. It is the key of the Grand Arcanum, the root of the Tree of Life, the science of Good and Evil." 2) "Therefore it must be re-vivified, and made to be born again from its ashes, which you will effect by virtue of the vegetation of the Tree of Life, represented to us by the branch of acacia. Whoever shall learn to comprehend and execute this great work, will know great things, say the Sages of the work; but whenever you depart from the centre of the Square and the Compass you will no longer be able to work with success." 3) "'Ye shall be like the Elohim, knowing good and evil,' had the Serpent of Genesis said, and the Tree of Knowledge became the Tree of Death. For six thousand years the Martyrs of Knowledge toil and die at the foot of this tree, that it may again become the Tree of Life."

I found 28 mentions in *Morals and Dogma* of the word Sephiroth and descriptions of its points and paths and their meaning. Consider this claim about *Morals and Dogma* on page 99: "There is in these few words a complete summary of the Theology of the Sephiroth." Pike writes that:

> All truly dogmatic religions have issued from the Kabalah and return to it: everything scientific and grand in the religious dreams of all the illuminati, Jacob Boehme, Swedenborg, Saint Martin, and others, is borrowed from the Kabalah; all the Masonic associations owe to it their Secrets and their Symbols. The Kabalah alone consecrates the alliance of the Universal Reason and the Divine Word; it establishes, by the counterpoises of two forces apparently opposite, the eternal balance of being; it alone reconciles Reason with Faith, Power with Liberty, Science with Mystery; it has the keys of the Present, the Past, and Future.

Another passage places the Sephiroth (points) of the Tree of Life as a core element of Masonic symbolism [emphasis added]:

> As such, it has revealed itself in ten emanations or Sephiroth, which are not ten different beings, nor even beings at all; but sources of life, vessels of Omnipotence, and types of Creation. They are Sovereignty or Will,

Wisdom, Intelligence, Benignity, Severity, Beauty, Victory, Glory, Permanency, and Empire. These are attributes of God; and this idea, that **God reveals Himself by His attributes, and that the human mind cannot perceive or discern God Himself, in his works, but only his mode of manifesting Himself, is a profound Truth**.

Pike expresses his deep affection for the Qabalah with this passage:

One is filled with admiration, on penetrating into the Sanctuary of the Kabalah, at seeing a doctrine so logical, so simple, and at the same time so absolute. The necessary union of ideas and signs, the consecration of the most fundamental realities by the primitive characters; the Trinity of Words, Letters, and Numbers; a philosophy simple as the alphabet, profound and infinite as the Word; theorems more complete and luminous than those of Pythagoras; a theology summed up by counting on one's fingers; an Infinite which can be held in the hollow of an infant's hand; ten ciphers, and twenty-two letters, a triangle, a square, and a circle,—these are all the elements of the Kabalah. These are the elementary principles of the written Word, reflection of that spoken Word that created the world! This is the doctrine of the Kabalah, with which you will no doubt seek to make yourself acquainted, as to the Creation.

In his book, *The Meaning of Masonry* (1922), self-professed Freemason of 32 years, W. L. Wilmshurst (British), writing officially on behalf of his Order, mentions the Tree of Life twice (that I found): 1) "And as the Angel stood with a flaming sword at the entrance of Eden to guard the way to the Tree of Life, so will the man whose initiation is not a conventional one find himself threatened at the door of the higher knowledge by opposing invisible forces if he rashly rushes forward in a state of moral unfitness into the deep secrets of the Centre." 2) "As the flaming sword is described as keeping the way to the Tree of Life from those as yet unfitted to approach it, so does the secret law of the Spirit still avenge itself upon those who are unqualified to participate in the knowledge of its mysteries." These passages relate to Genesis 3:22-24.[24]

Manly Hall, a 33° Scottish Rite Freemason and noted writer on the "Mysteries" (ancient initiation societies that are the philosophic predecessors to Freemasonry), in *The Secret Teachings of All Ages* (1928), ascribes a near universal meaning to the Tree of Life [emphasis added]:

---

[24] 3x22 = 66. 3x24 = 72. See Figure 2 (360-294=66, 360-288=72).

Though humanity is still wandering in a world of good and evil, it will ultimately attain completion and eat of the fruit of the Tree of Life growing in the midst of the illusionary **garden of worldly things**. Thus the Tree of Life is also the appointed symbol of the Mysteries [of which Freemasonry is one], and by partaking of its fruit man attains immortality.

Hall makes the following claim about the oak tree specifically, which I equate with the Oak Island Tree of Life: "The Father God of the Mysteries was often worshiped under the form of an oak." This point suggests a possible harmony symbolized by the Oak Island Tree of Life. Pike notes several times in *Morals and Dogma* that humans cannot observe God himself, but only his emanations, those aspects of the Deity by which He chooses to reveal Himself (see quote above). In the Mysteries, Pike claims, those emanations have certain properties, some linked to sexual characteristics of humans, and that those "sexual characteristics are symbolically assigned." God is neither male, nor female, nor both, but reveals emanations of Himself that humans symbolically link to gender. Anyway, if the "Father God" (emanation linked to male attributes) is worshipped under an oak, then the Oak Island Tree of Life reflects the male gender. The Tree of Life template on Oak Island has an 8-by-5 ratio to its dimensions (8x144-by-5x144). This ratio is also the ratio of Venus's orbit to Earth's orbit. For every eight orbits of Venus around the Sun, the Earth orbits five times (8 Venus years equals 5 Earth years; not exactly, but quite close). This is the reason that Venus is linked with the pentagram (the five-pointed star). If Venus's position relative to the Sun is marked on the same day each year for five years, then those points form a pentagram. As such, the 8-by-5 ratio of the Tree of Life might indicate Venus (a feminine emanation of the Deity). This gives us the male and female in one shape. We'll return later to the TOL template and its connection with Venus, but for now make a mental note that the center column of the TOL, which has a length of 8x144 feet, is the part corresponding to Venus. The width of the TOL, having a length of 5x144 feet, corresponds to Earth (material). These two paths are perpendicular to one another.

Of cedar, which I observe to be used interchangeably by Freemasons with the acacia and other evergreens, Hall writes: "Among the ancient Egyptians and Jews the acacia, or tamarisk, was held in the highest religious esteem; and among modern Masons, branches of acacia, cypress, cedar, or evergreen are still regarded as most significant emblems." Hall offers four possible symbolisms for acacia (cedar). The three that seem most relevant to our current quest are: 1) "it is the emblem of the vernal equinox—the annual resurrection of the solar deity;" 2) "it fittingly typifies human immortality and regeneration, and under the form of the evergreen represents that immortal part of man which survives the destruction of his visible nature;" and 3) "it is the ancient and revered emblem of the Mysteries, and candidates entering the tortuous passageways in which the ceremonials were given carried in their hands branches of these sacred plants." Wilmshurst echoes this symbolism of initiation: "...in the reference to the sprig of acacia planted at the head of the grave of the Masonic Grand Master and prototype, Hiram Abiff. The grave is the candidate's soul; the sprig of acacia typifies the latent akasa (to use an Eastern term) or divine germ planted in that soil and waiting to become quickened into activity in his intelligence, the 'head' [skull] of that plane."

Hall then ties acacia to the central figure in Freemasonry, Hiram Abiff, the supposed architect of Soloman's Temple, and a figure that is murdered and resurrected in ritualistic Freemasonry. Hall uses the name CHiram for Hiram Abiff.

As the legend of CHiram Abiff is based upon the ancient Egyptian Mystery ritual of the murder and resurrection of Osiris, it is natural that the sprig of acacia [cedar] should be preserved as symbolic of the resurrection of CHiram. The chest containing the body of Osiris was washed ashore near Byblos and lodged in the roots of a tamarisk, or acacia, which, growing into a mighty tree, enclosed within its trunk the body of the murdered god. This is undoubtably the origin of the story that a sprig of acacia marks the grave of CHiram.

Cedar is also mentioned many times in the Bible, such as 2 Samuel 5:11: "And Hiram king of Tyre sent messengers to David, and cedar trees, and carpenters, and masons: and they built David a house."

I think that this laundry list of references sufficiently validates the inclusion of the Tree of Life and cedar as key symbols within Freemasonry. It is more than plausible that Freemasons would use this collection of symbols (Tree of Life, cedar, oak) to create their secret map. This idea will be bolstered later when we decipher the map. Now, let's return to the George Washington Masonic National Memorial.

The Cedar Branch

We arrived at the George Washington Masonic National Memorial (GW MM) by following the winter solstice azimuth. Along a rhumb line, the Newport Tower and point [10] on the GW MM TOL are 356.2177511 miles apart, approximately. By continuing that southwesterly 238.76-degree azimuth from the GW MM we find ourselves in the American South. I did not find any Masonic symbolism in that direction. At the GW MM, the sun rises on the summer solstice over the Newport Tower (from whence we came). It sets on the summer solstice at an azimuth of 301.4 degrees (northwest). If we follow that bearing for 356 miles (i.e., the same distance as from the Newport Tower), then we find ourselves in Lake Erie. Back track five miles and you are in the middle of Sandusky, Ohio. I almost stopped my investigation there. Clearly my theory was falling apart. I'd never heard of the place. But, an unquenchable thirst for the Truth propelled me forward. Either that or a mildly obsessive personality and a lack of weekend plans.

First, I noticed that my solstice line passed through a park in the center of Sandusky, Washington Park, centered at the intersection of Washington St and Columbus Ave. So, we have the George Washington Masonic Memorial to Washington Park in the heart of—what was it called again?—Sandusky, OH. But, there's a Washington Park in every town in America. So what?

I then observed that in the southwest corner of the park there is a triangle-shaped city block that appeared to be a 3-4-5 right triangle. Our background in geometry tells us that a 3-4-5 triangle is a right triangle with sides of length 3, 4, and 5, or multiples thereof. The Pythagorean theorem tells us that 9 + 16 = 25 forms a right triangle. Anyway, remember what I said about Freemasons being geometry nerds. The 3-4-5 triangle is a central symbol in their philosophy and rituals. I used Google Earth to measure the sidewalks and it was indeed a 3-4-5 right triangle, with the shortest side having a length of 147 feet (a core dimension of the Oak Island Tree of Life).[25] The Pythagorean theorem is often known as Pythagoras's Proposition 1:47.[26] Now I was interested.

I then started searching for a place to put the 1152-foot long Tree of Life template. When I placed point [10] on the "X" at the end of the sidewalk on the 147-foot leg and aligned the center column with that sidewalk, it ended 1152 feet away at the street curb that borders the opposite end of the park (along Adams St). This placed the TOL on a bearing of 66 degrees from point [10] to point [1]. The points on the right column (points [2], [4], [7]) do not appear to coincide with any identifiable markers, but point [3] sat atop some ornate bushes, point [8] sat atop a fountain that is an attraction of the park, path [4]-[5] overlaid a sidewalk (along Columbus Ave), and path [7]-[8] passed down a walkway and through the center of the government building adjacent to the park. The major items in the park, such as the fountain, the gazebo, and others were aligned along the left column of the TOL 360 feet from the sidewalk that forms the center column.

If the left column, path [8]-[3], were extended in the direction of the top of the TOL it would bisect a large Compass and Square Masonic emblem, artfully crafted, that sits in the northeastern corner (the Masonic cornerstone) of the park. It faces east. Across the street from this Masonic emblem is the Masonic Temple, Science Lodge 50, which was chartered in 1818, a few months before the town of Sandusky.

If one zooms out a smidgen from their closeup of downtown Sandusky, they will observe two roads with the word cedar in their names. This is because Sandusky, OH is the home to Cedar Point, which has been an amusement park since the 1800s. To my eye, Cedar Point juts from the mainland looking very much like the branch of cedar held by our Beautiful

---

[25] I measured along the inset sidewalks, not the adjacent roads.
[26] http://www.themathpage.com/abooki/propi-47.htm

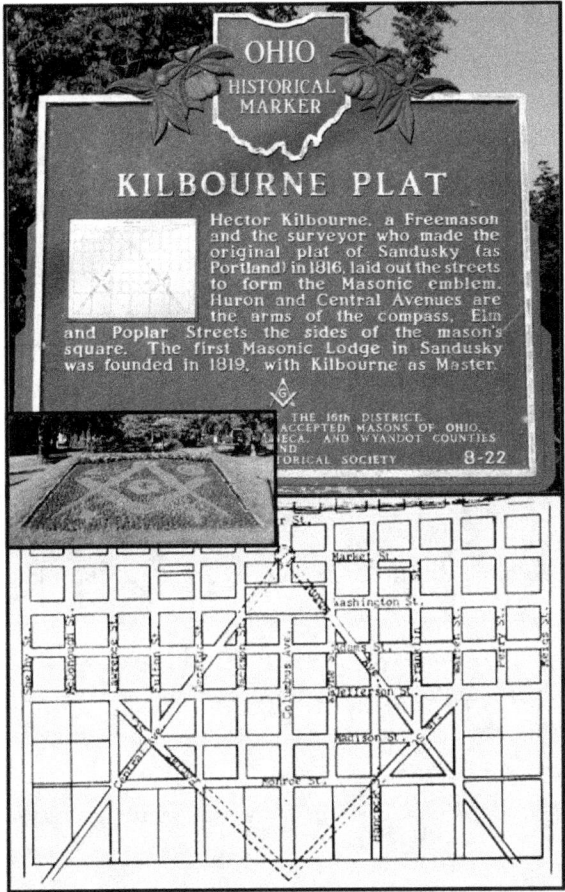

Figure 9: Kilbourne Plat, Historical Marker, Compass & Square display.

Virgin (Figure 8). The roads are Cedar Point Rd and Cedar Point Dr, and they begin in almost perfect alignment with the summer solstice path that led us from the GW MM to Sandusky.

The roots of Freemasonry in Sandusky run deeper than these TOL similarities and a 3-4-5 triangle. Near the Masonic display in Washington Park is a historical marker entitled "Kilbourne Plat" that reads:

Hector Kilbourne, a Freemason and the surveyor who made the original plat of Sandusky (as Portland) in 1816, laid out the streets to form the Masonic emblem. Huron and Central Avenues are the arms of the compass. Elm and Poplar Streets the sides of the mason's square. The first Masonic Lodge in Sandusky was founded in 1818, with Kilbourne as Master.

Science Lodge 50 observes on its website that "Sandusky's unique square and compasses design is the only known occurrence of Masonic symbolism intentionally incorporated within any city in the world." Note, however, that the streets do not seem to currently adhere to this plan, although its remnants are clearly visible.

*****

I am asserting through my research that Sandusky is part of a larger Masonic structure, one that reaches now from the Newport Tower to the George Washington Masonic National Memorial to Washington Park at the top of Kilbourne's compass in Sandusky. But how can a land surveyor in Ohio be part of a plan that, in 1818, spanned a broad swath of the northern United States?

Hector Kilbourne was not born in Ohio. He was born in Connecticut. Sandusky, Cleveland, and the northern portion of Ohio were settled by the Connecticut Western Reserve (a company established to help settle the Ohio territory) and its offshoots. Hector moved to Ohio with his father James Kilbourne in 1803. In 1805, James Kilbourne was appointed United States surveyor of public lands.[27] An 1826 map of the Western Reserve lands labels Cedar Point as "Cedar Point," so this name was contemporary with the Kilbournes.[28]

The TOL layout in Sandusky's Washington Park is not as remarkable to me as the matches observed on the GW MM grounds, but when combined with Cedar Point, the Masonic pattern in the city streets, the solstice alignment with the GW MM, and James Kilbourne's position as United States surveyor, I feel that Sandusky and Cedar Point clearly fit within this overall Masonic architecture.

The reader should also note that if one travels up the Cedar Point branch, not quite to the northern tip (stop at mini golf), they reach 41.485818 degrees latitude, which is exactly west of the Newport Tower. In other words, at Cedar Point, Ohio, the sun rises on the equinoxes over the Newport Tower, and at the Newport Tower, the sun sets on the equinoxes over Cedar Point, Ohio. So, our path, starting at the Newport Tower, follows sunset in

---

[27] http://en.wikipedia.org/wiki/James_Kilbourne

[28] http://upload.wikimedia.org/wikipedia/commons/8/8b/ Western_Reserve_Including_the_Fire_Lands_1826.jpg

the winter, sunset in the summer, and sunrise in the spring. A marker for this east-west alignment might be in Cleveland where our east-west line passes a quarter-mile south of Cedar St, which runs perfectly east-west. Recall Hall's explanation for a symbolic meaning of cedar: "it is the emblem of the vernal [spring] equinox—the annual resurrection of the solar deity."

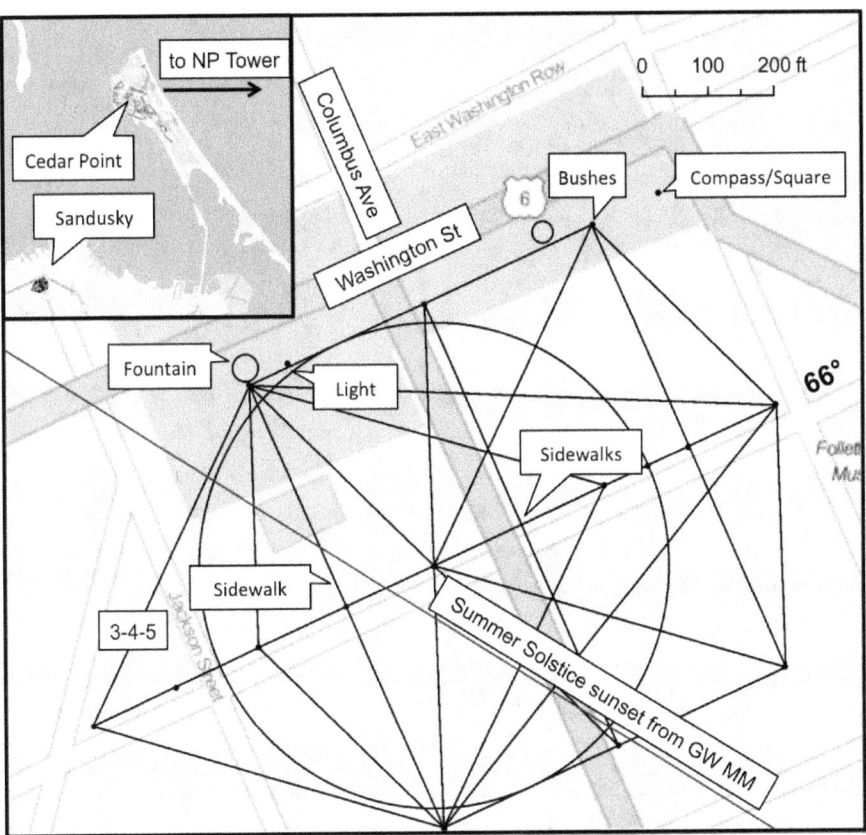

Figure 10: Sandusky and its Tree of Life; Cedar Point.

The Chalice

The pattern that we have created thus far by connecting the Newport Tower, the GW MM, and Cedar Point, Ohio, forms a downward "V" shape. In Alexandria, VA where King St intersects the Potomac, 1.5 miles from the GW MM, is an interesting sidewalk shape. It appears to be a martini glass, or chalice. I doubt that it is related to our quest, but it sparked an idea: does our downward "V" shape have a stem? Perhaps a clue to this question can be found in the engraving of the Virgin and Father Time (Figure 8) that is part of Freemasonry's initiation for the Third Degree. Directly above Father Time's pointing finger, but not in the direction that he is pointing, is a backwards lowercase Greek letter xi (ξ). This character was used by the Greeks to represent the number 60. So, perhaps a backwards character means -60. Regardless, we have used two paths to connect our sites thus far: rounding up a degree, the Newport Tower is on a 60-degree azimuth from the GW MM. In the reverse direction this is 240 degrees. Cedar Point, Ohio is 300 degrees (rounded from 301 degrees) from the GW MM. In the opposite direction this is 120 degrees back to the GW MM. So, we have 60, 120, 240, and 300 degrees being used. The only remaining orientations that are increments of 60 are north (0) and south (180). So, let's look down the stem of our chalice, the stem of our Y. What is 180 degrees from the GW MM and beneath the sun at high noon?

If you travel due south from the GW MM you will eventually hit the ocean at a beach town named Cedar Point, North Carolina. Travel about 1000 feet west on Cedar Point Blvd and you will encounter Masonic Ave. Turn right up Masonic Ave and you will immediately see a sign with a Masonic emblem on it that advertises a site at the end of Masonic Ave called the Jones Masonic Campus, which despite a dearth of information available on the Internet appears to be a retirement community still under development.

Surely, the rowdy beach town of Cedar Point, NC must be a modern invention and not in some way part of the original layout of our fine nation. According to the town's website: "In 1713, King George III issued a land grant of 2080 acres located in Western Carteret County known as Cedar Point to Thomas Lee of Virginia."[29] The town seal claims "est. 1713." Thomas Lee is the ancestor of Robert E. Lee and is a dominant figure in the pre-history of the United States. His descendants had close ties to the Washington family,

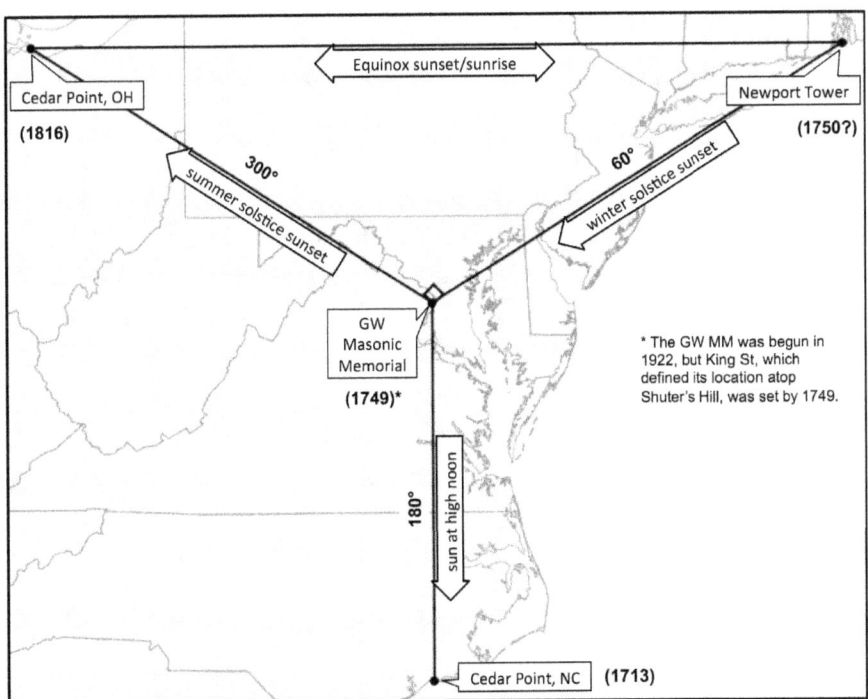

Figure 11: The Chalice (120-degree Y-shape), DC diamond at its center.

---

[29] http://www.cedarpointnc.org/cedar-point-nc-history.php

as they were both prominent in northern Virginia. And it just so happens that the 2080 acres that he acquired, of the 31.12 million acres in North Carolina, were directly south of where the GW MM currently stands, and was known as Cedar Point. To me, this cannot be a coincidence.

Cedar Point's website also claims: "The western half of Cedar Point passed through four generations of Hills family. The famous Octagon House, built by Edward Hill, is located in this area. It was finished in 1859 on the Hill Plantation. Built by shipwrights, it has proven its durability surviving the test of time." The Octagon House, which was donated to Freemasons in 1999, is located on what is now the Jones Masonic Campus.[30] Oddly, if one travels along a bearing of 279 degrees—the bearing of the GW MM TOL—from the Octagon House then they will run into the Scottish Rite Temple in Charlotte, NC.

This concludes the first part of our investigation, as we have created a complete shape using our theory (see Figure 11). That theory used the Oak Island Tree of Life as a vector, i.e., looking along the paths created by its segments, and used the sun as a vector. We started at Oak Island and followed the center column of its Tree of Life to the Newport Tower. From there we followed the sunset azimuth on the winter solstice to a Tree of Life at the George Washington Masonic National Memorial. Cedar St marks this Tree of Life. We then followed the sunset azimuth on the summer solstice to the Masonic-designed streets of Sandusky, Ohio and another Tree of Life. This Tree of Life was marked by Cedar Point. We then noted that sunrise and sunset azimuths on the equinoxes connect Cedar Point, Ohio and the Newport Tower. Last, we followed the azimuth of the sun at high-noon (due south) from the GW MM to Cedar Point, North Carolina and a Masonic Campus. Together, these points create a Y shape with the GW MM in the middle; the Newport Tower at 60 degrees from the GW MM; Cedar Point, NC at 180 degrees from the GW MM; and Cedar Point, OH at 300 degrees from the GW MM. These angles (60, 180, 300) are all separated by 120 degrees. The GW MM is home to Masonic Lodge 120. But this Y shape (chalice) is only part of the overall map. To discover the rest we must depart from our initial theory and do some general exploration. But first, let's take a moment to better understand the craftsmen of this plan. Who are the Freemasons, and what is Freemasonry?

---

[30] http://beaufortartist.blogspot.com/2008/01/beauforts-connection-to-octagon-house.html

The Order of the Quest

Freemasonry is a fraternity within a fraternity—an outer organization concealing an inner brotherhood of the elect. Before it is possible to intelligently discuss the origin of the craft it is necessary to establish the existence of these two separate yet interdependent orders, the one visible and the other invisible.[31]

    - Manly Hall, 33° Scottish Rite Freemason

Freemasonry is a not-so-secret society formed of several different orders, thousands of lodges, and millions of members worldwide. In the United States there are a few million Freemasons of various orders. The basic garden variety, meat-and-potatoes Freemasonry, called Craft or Blue Masonry, consists of members seeking to complete initiation in the three levels of Freemasonry: Entered Apprentice, Fellowcraft, and Master Mason. Other versions of Freemasonry, such as the Scottish and York Rites, offer "higher" degrees than these three, but in reality, there is no Mason superior to a Master Mason. The website of the Scottish Rite, which has 33 degrees, puts these higher degrees in perspective.[32] It reads: "Before you can join the Scottish Rite, you first must become a Master Mason [at a Blue Lodge].... While there

---

[31] Hall, Manly P. (1929) *Lectures on Ancient Philosophy.*

[32] http://scottishrite.org/about/how-to-join/

is no Masonic degree more important than that of Master Mason, there is a long tradition—almost as old as Freemasonry—of 'high degrees' that expand upon and elaborate the teachings and lessons of the first three degrees." These teachings involve rituals that use mason's tools (e.g., compass, square, and level), astronomy, and other devices as symbols reflecting lessons of self-improvement (to understate it), and "truths" about humanity and the universe. Albert Pike wrote [emphasis in original]:

> Christianity taught the doctrine of FRATERNITY; but repudiated that of political EQUALITY, by continually inculcating obedience to Caesar, and to those lawfully in authority. Masonry was the first apostle of EQUALITY. In the Monastery there is fraternity and equality, but no liberty. Masonry added that also, and claimed for man the three-fold heritage, LIBERTY, EQUALITY, and FRATERNITY.

I will introduce here, and revisit throughout the book, two aspects of our investigation into Freemasonry: who are Freemasons (the persons), and what is Freemasonry (the craft). Debates persist within Freemasonry about basic and not-so-basic principles, to include schisms among Orders pertaining to the role of religion and the place of God in its teachings and initiations. The reader will be well served to consider Freemasonry (the persons and the craft) to be a large, complex, and multifaceted fraternity of different personalities and ideals, each person having their own understanding of Masonry.

"The government hates rap," declared comedian Chris Rock. His humorous intent and underlying point aside, these words are absurd. The "government" does not exist as a single-minded, monolithic being. It is composed of many persons, some liberal, some conservative, some smart, some less so, some hard-working, some less so, some kind and empathetic, some less so, and so on. There are employees of "the government" that enjoy rap and others that do not, at all levels. Freemasonry is similarly mischaracterized as a monolithic entity, of a single mind with a single plan and a single belief system. Truth is not served by such generalizations. During its history, Freemasons have been among society's most revered (George Washington) and among those deserving of far less respect. Masonic writers, such as Albert Pike and W. L. Wilmshurst, lament in their works the behaviors of some Masons that have acted poorly, at times evoking the name of the Order in their selfish cause. Compare these bad apples to police officers or other government officials that attempt to gain special access or avoid punishment by citing their positions: "You can't make me wait in line like everyone else, I'm the mayor." As you continue to research Freemasonry (or any other sizable group), I recommend that you not judge it by its best or worst members. Yet, the Freemasons that I am implicating in this book do fit a general demographic: affluent white males of Protestant upbringing. That was the predominant demographic of Freemasonry in early U.S. history. Orders catering to other demographics were formed to overcome these barriers. For example:

> Prince Hall Freemasonry exists because of the refusal of early American lodges to admit African-Americans. In 1775, an African-American named Prince Hall, along with fourteen other African-Americans, was initiated into a British military lodge with a warrant from the Grand Lodge of Ireland, having failed to obtain admission from the other lodges in Boston.[33]

Albert Pike, a former head of the American Scottish Rite (Southern Jurisdiction), for all his words of freedom and equality, still acted in defense of slavery, as was common to an American southerner during his time: "I am not one of those who believe slavery a blessing. I know it is an evil,... The Negro will be free in God's good time; and the coming of that time we cannot hasten."[34] But he did not find himself as helpless amid God's plan as these words suggest; he lifted more than a finger in the face of slavery and served the Confederate Army. Perhaps he feared the repercussions of challenging the status quo. The fear of death can be a powerful motivator.

Some become Freemasons because of its social gatherings, others because of reputation, and others because of its mystery. Many reasons exist for persons to join. What, then, is the original purpose of Freemasonry? Persons at some point in the past expended great effort to devise a deep system of symbols and rituals, but for what purpose? To explore this question, I will rely heavily on two sources, both already quoted at some length: *The Meaning Of Masonry* (1922), by W. L. Wilmshurst, and *Morals and Dogma* (1871), by Albert Pike. For 100 years, initiates of the American Scottish Rite were given a copy of *Morals and Dogma* as study material. It is still recommended reading. I consider it a deliberately confusing, but authoritative source. *The Meaning of Masonry* (of the York Rite) is more direct and less symbolically comprehensive, but also is authoritative. Rather than

---

[33] https://en.wikipedia.org/wiki/Freemasonry

[34] http://www.phoenixmasonry.org/masonicmuseum/albert_pike_statue_in_washington_dc.htm

burdening the reader with my own stilted efforts to paraphrase these and other texts, I will quote them heavily and stitch together a portrait of Freemasonry at the surface level. I will add bolding to the quotes so as to highlight words important to our purpose here, while preserving for the reader the context around these passages. In a few lengthy sentences, Wilmshurst describes the members of the Order:

> The Order is a semi-secret, semi-public institution; secret in respect of its activities intra mœnia, but otherwise of full public notoriety, with its doors open to any applicant for admission who is of ordinary good character and repute. Those who enter it, as the majority do, entirely ignorant of what they will find there, usually because they have friends there or know Masonry to be an institution devoted to high ideals and benevolence and with which it may be socially desirable to be connected, may or may not be attracted and profit by what is disclosed to them, and may or may not see anything beyond the bare form of the symbol or hear anything beyond the mere letter of the word. Their admission is quite a lottery; their Initiation too often remains but a formality, not an actual awakening into an order and quality of life previously unexperienced; their membership, unless such an awakening eventually ensues from the careful study and faithful practice of the Order's teaching, has little, if any, greater influence upon them than would ensue from their joining a purely social club.

Wilmshurst articulates the scope of Freemasonry: "It is absurd to think that a vast organization like Masonry was ordained merely to teach to grown-up men of the world the symbolical meaning of a few simple builders' tools, or to impress upon us such elementary virtues as temperance and justice." He notes that "the children in every village school are taught such things; or to enforce such simple principles of morals as brotherly love, which every church and every religion teaches; or as relief, which is practised quite as much by non-Masons as by us; or of truth, which every infant learns upon its mother's knee." The effort put into creating the philosophy and rituals of Freemasonry suggests a deeper purpose. **It is these original craftsmen of Masonry, and not contemporary Freemasons, that are most important to our quest.** Wilmshurst continues:

> There is surely, too, no need for us to join a secret society to be taught that the volume of the Sacred Law is a fountain of truth and instruction; or to go through the great and elaborate ceremony of the third degree

merely to learn that we have each to die. The Craft whose work we are
taught to honour with the name of a 'science,' a 'royal art,' has surely
some larger end in view than merely inculcating the practice of social
virtues common to all the world and by no means the monopoly of
Freemasons.

But Freemasonry does not solve this riddle for its members. Freemasons are
not given during their progression through its ranks a cheatsheet on its true
meaning. Rather, they are given a figurative codebook of symbols to
decipher. Pike [emphasis added]:

> It is for each individual Mason to discover the secret of Masonry, by
> reflection upon its symbols and a wise consideration and analysis of what
> is said and done in the work. **Masonry does not inculcate her truths**.
> She states them, once and briefly; or hints them, perhaps, darkly; or
> interposes a cloud between them and eyes that would be dazzled by
> them. 'Seek, and ye shall find,' knowledge and the truth.

But what truth? Wilmshurst sets up the quest:

> Surely, then, it behoves us to acquaint ourselves with what that larger
> end consists, to enquire why the fulfilment of that purpose is worthy to
> be called a science, and to ascertain what are those 'mysteries' to which
> our doctrine promises we may ultimately attain if we apply ourselves
> assiduously enough to understanding what Masonry is capable of
> teaching us. Realizing, then, what Masonry cannot be deemed to be, let
> us ask what it is.

The reader should retain during our journey that secrecy was considered
paramount to Masonry's construct. If the "truth" that Freemasonry offers its
most astute members is as widely indisputable as astronomical fact, then
secrecy would be unnecessary. Secrecy here has a purpose. Wilmshurst
[emphasis added]:

> In all periods of the world's history, and in every part of the globe, secret
> orders and societies have existed **outside the limits of the official
> churches** for the purpose of teaching what are called 'the Mysteries': for
> imparting to **suitable and prepared minds** certain truths of human life,
> certain instructions about divine things, about the things that belong to
> our peace, about human nature and **human destiny**, which it was
> **undesirable to publish to the multitude** who would but profane those
> teachings and apply the esoteric knowledge that was communicated to
> perverse and perhaps to disastrous ends.

Wilmshurst includes a wide and timeless list of persons in this history. I leave it to the reader to determine the historical truth of these claims, but I'll note that this sort of claim is common in Masonic literature and teachings.

> All the great teachers of humanity, Socrates, Plato, Pythagoras, Moses, Aristotle, Virgil , the author of the Homeric poems, and the great Greek tragedians, along with St. John, St. Paul and innumerable other great names—were initiates of the Sacred Mysteries. The form of the teaching communicated has varied considerably from age to age; it has been expressed under different veils; but since the ultimate truth the Mysteries aim at teaching is always one and the same, there has always been taught, and can only be taught, one and the same doctrine. What that doctrine was, and still is, we will consider presently so far as we are able to speak of it, and so far as Masonry gives expression to it. For the moment let me merely say that **behind all the official religious systems of the world**, and behind all the great moral movements and developments in the history of humanity, have stood what St. Paul called **the keepers or 'stewards of the Mysteries.'** [emphasis added]

Pike [emphasis added]: "The Hebrew books [Old Testament] were written only to recall to memory the traditions; and they **were written in Symbols unintelligible to the Profane** [uninitiated person]." The "profane" are those persons that find literal meaning in these symbols, such as those that worshipped an idol of Zeus or Apollo, or who believed that the Sun was an actual god, rather than an inanimate object adopted as a symbol of life-giving power and intellectual development.

Has Freemasonry itself been hidden behind the development of these religious doctrines? Wilmshurst thinks not:

> I wish to emphasize at this stage... that our present system is not one coming from remote antiquity: that there is no direct continuity between us [modern Freemasons] and the Egyptians, or even those ancient Hebrews who built, in the reign of King Solomon, a certain Temple at Jerusalem. What is extremely ancient in Freemasonry is the spiritual doctrine concealed within the architectural phraseology [masonic symbols]; for this doctrine is an elementary form of the doctrine that has been taught in all ages, no matter in what garb it has been expressed. Our own teaching, for instance, recognizes Pythagoras as having undergone numerous initiations in different parts of the world, and as having attained great eminence in the science. Now it is perfectly certain

that Pythagoras was not a Mason at all in our present sense of the word;
but it is also perfectly certain that Pythagoras was a very highly advanced
master in the knowledge of the secret schools of the Mysteries, of whose
doctrine some small portion is enshrined for us in our Masonic system.

I have touched on two aspects of our question about Freemasonry: the
first being the purpose of Freemasonry, and the second being its means to
that end. Pike offers this on the former [emphasis added]:

> The practical object of Masonry is the physical and moral amelioration
> and the intellectual and spiritual improvement of individuals and society.
> Neither can be effected, except by the **dissemination of truth. It is
> falsehood in doctrines and fallacy in principles, to which most of
> the miseries of men and the misfortunes of nations are owing.
> Public opinion is rarely right on any point**; and there are and always
> will be important truths to be substituted in that opinion in the place of
> many errors and absurd and injurious prejudices. **There are few truths
> that public opinion has not at some time hated and persecuted as
> heresies; and few errors that have not at some time seemed to it
> truths radiant from the immediate presence of God.**

I have found Pike's claim to be made consistently by Masonic writers, that
Freemasonry aims to teach persons to better themselves (spiritually and
morally), and thus better society, through their pains-taken acquisition of
certain "truths" that are held in secret to prevent their discovery (and
disruption) by unprepared persons, often called the vulgar or the profane.
We'll return to these ideas as we uncover elements of this plan, but for now,
keep in mind that the truths of Freemasonry are buried (deliberately) in
symbolism as a means of concealing them from the uninitiated. Freemasons
speak of tools (aprons, ploughs, squares, compasses, etc.) because they have
symbolic meaning, and *only* because they have symbolic meaning. Masonic
literature stomps its proverbial foot on the ground saying of these tools,
"which we use symbolically," hoping that its members will begin to free their
minds from the material purpose of these tools. **If you take any words of
Freemasonry at face value (i.e., literally) then you are missing the point.**
I find that a sizable portion of Freemasonry's negative reputation stems from
this sort of misunderstanding. I'll annotate this passage from Pike to illustrate
one level of symbolism [foot-stomping emphasis in original]:

> A rough Ashlar is the shapeless stone [given to new initiates,
> representing themselves] which is to be prepared in order to commence

the philosophical work; and to be developed, in order to change its form from triangular to cubic [perfection], after the separation from it of its Salt, Sulphur, and Mercury [human impurities], by the aid of the Square, Level, Plumb, and Balance [crafting and measuring tools], and all the other Masonic implements *which we use symbolically*.

Pike notes that [emphasis added]:

Masonry, like all the Religions, all the Mysteries, Hermeticism and Alchemy, conceals its secrets from all except the Adepts and Sages, or the Elect, and **uses false explanations and misinterpretations of its symbols to mislead** those who deserve only to be misled; to conceal **the Truth, which it calls Light**, from them, and to draw them away from it. Truth is not for those who are unworthy or unable to receive it, or would pervert it.... Every age has had a religion suited to its capacity.

He continues: "The Teachers, even of Christianity, are, in general, the most ignorant of the true meaning of that which they teach. There is no book of which so little is known as the Bible. To most who read it, it is as incomprehensible as the [Qabalah]." Pike is praising the Bible, but not those who claim to follow it. Pike then warns the initiates: "Masonry jealously conceals its secrets, and intentionally leads conceited interpreters astray." Freemasonry seems to be wary of the common man, and perhaps rightly so. The Earth was not the center of the Universe until the Church capitulated otherwise, and yet Galileo regardless was persecuted (by the Church and its followers) for stating an objective Truth. His opponents believed that they understood, or even spoke on behalf of, an infinitely complex God that no doubt was aware of the Earth's rotation around the Sun. It is from these zealots, who mistake belief for Truth (sometimes violently), that Freemasonry seems to direct its barrier of misinformation. This suggests that Freemasonry's secrets challenge (or "clarify") beliefs commonly held by the religious. Wilmshurst [emphasis added]:

Masonry offers us, in dramatic form and by means of dramatic ceremonial a philosophy of the spiritual life of man and a diagram of the process of regeneration. We shall see presently that that philosophy is not only consistent with the doctrine of every religious system taught outside the ranks of the Order, but that it explains, **elucidates and more sharply defines**, the fundamental doctrines common to every religious system in the world, whether past or present, whether Christian or non-Christian. The religions of the world, though all aiming at teaching truth, express that truth in different ways, and we [Masons] are more prone to emphasize the differences than to look for the correspondences in what they teach. In some Masonic Lodges the candidate makes his first entrance to the Lodge room amid the clash of swords and the sounds of strife, to intimate to him that he is leaving the confusion and jarring of the religious sects of the exterior world, and is passing into a Temple wherein the Brethren dwell together in unity of thought in regard to the basal truths of life, truths which can permit of no difference or schism.

So what, again, is Freemasonry? Pike [capitalization in original, other emphasis added]:

You have heard more than one definition of Freemasonry. The truest and the most significant you have yet to hear.... FREEMASONRY is the subjugation of the Human that is in man by the Divine; **the Conquest of the Appetites and Passions by the Moral Sense and the Reason**; a continual effort, struggle, and warfare of **the Spiritual against the Material and Sensual**. That victory, when it has been achieved and secured, and the conqueror may rest upon his shield and wear the well-earned laurels, is the true HOLY EMPIRE. To achieve it, the Mason must first attain a solid conviction, **founded upon reason**, that he hath within him **a spiritual nature, a soul that is not to die when the body is dissolved**, but is to continue to exist and to advance toward perfection through all the ages of eternity, and to see more and more clearly, as it draws nearer unto God, the Light of the Divine Presence.

We will return to this definition later, but recall that nothing is to be taken literally. To the creators of Freemasonry, the word "spirit" here means something different than what it might mean to you. Wilmshurst offers his own purpose for Freemasonry:

It proclaims the fact that there exists a higher and more secret path of life than that which we normally tread, and that when the outer world and its pursuits and rewards lose their attractiveness for us and prove insufficient to our deeper needs, as sooner or later they will, we are compelled to turn back upon ourselves, to seek and knock at the door of a world within; and it is upon this inner world, and the path to and through it, that Masonry promises light, charts the way, and indicates the qualifications and conditions of progress. This is the sole aim and intention of Masonry.

Is the reader to take from all of this that hidden behind Freemasonry's symbols is a doctrine that they [Masons] want the reader to believe? No. Unlike many (or most) religions, Freemasons do not proselytize; that is, they do not recruit others to their Order or to their philosophy. They are dissuaded from doing so. Wilmshurst [emphasis in original]:

> The reason why no man should be solicited to join the Order is that in regard to these matters of sacred and momentous import, the first springs of impulse must originate within the postulant himself; the first place of his preparation *must* ever be in his own heart, and it is to the cry and knocking of his inward need, and for no less a motive, that—in theory, though scarcely in practice—the door to the Mysteries is opened and the seeker enters in and finds help.

Although, Wilmshurst and others acknowledge the obvious reality that some Masons might suggest or urge friends and family to become Masons, just as one might promote a local social club or their favorite hobby. But this behavior is quite different from, say, a Mormon knocking on your front door to share their faith, and is entirely different from the "convert or die" mentality of Catholic Conquistadores and Islamic extremists.

Wilmshurst notes that new initiates to Freemasonry find "a certain religious element in it, but as they are told that religious discussion, which means, of course, sectarian religious discussion, is forbidden in the Lodge, they infer that Masonry is not a religious institution, and that its [Freemasonry's] teachings are intended to be merely secondary and supplemental to any religious tenets they [the initiate] may happen to hold."

Let's return to our map-making. There is a treasure left hidden for us to find. We'll venture next to Washington DC, the site of the Capital, despite Thomas Jefferson's preference to place it on Shuter's Hill, where the George Washington Masonic National Memorial now stands.

The Eye

I first demonstrated the application of the Tree of Life template at the George Washington Masonic National Memorial, an obvious candidate for Masonic influence, and then we rushed off to exciting and immortal places like Cedar Point, OH and Cedar Point, NC. What about other obvious candidate locations, such as nearby Washington DC? We'll take this detour because deep down we all knew that DC was part of the plan.

If you place point [10] of the Tree of Life at the intersection of 16th and H Streets NW, on the northern border of Lafayette Square, which is adjacent to the White House, and you orient the TOL to the south (180 degrees) from point [10] you will observe the following alignments (Figure 12). Point [9] is in the center of Lafayette Square. Points [7] and [8] corner the statues (in Lafayette Square) of General Lafayette and Jean Baptiste Rochambeau. The path connecting points [4] and [5] crosses the fountain in the north lawn. The Knowledge point is at the northern edge of the White House (the front overhang). The buried stone point overlays the President's desk in the Oval Office. Point [2] is at the outer edge of the West Wing. In other words, the west side of the White House is 360 feet wide, as is our TOL. Point [3] is at a gate, since the East Wing is shorter than the West Wing. Recall that the TOL

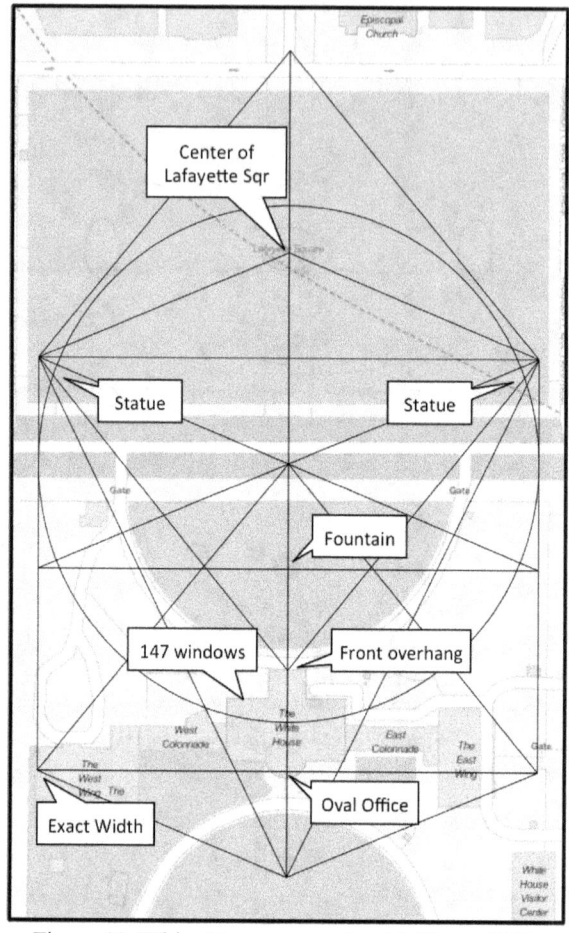

Figure 12: White House grounds with Tree of Life

template has four segments along its center column 147 feet in length. Oddly, the White House has 147 windows to bring Light inside.[35]

This alignment is interesting, but I suspect that it indicates a larger arrangement. One of the threads worth exploring is the use of the TOL length (1152 feet) as a basic unit of measurement. For example, the distance from the center of the Pentagon to the center of the Capital dome is 13 Tree of Life units (1 TOL unit = 1152 feet). In other words, it's 13-times the length of the Oak Island Tree of Life (13.00x1152 feet). I found another set of measurements more interesting. At the corner of 16th and S Streets NW is the conspicuous headquarters of Scottish Rite Freemasonry: The Scottish Rite of Freemasonry, Supreme Council, 33°, Southern Jurisdiction, U.S.A.

---

[35] http://en.wikipedia.org/wiki/White_House#Layout_and_amenities

Freemasons call this building "The House of the Temple." To avoid lengthy titles, I shall refer to this building as Scottish Rite HQ. The distance from this building to the White House is 5x1152 feet. Its distance to the U.S. Capital Building is 10x1152 feet, or twice its distance to the White House. I noticed that the distance from point [10] on the TOL to point [9] is 282 feet and the distance from point [10] to point [8] is 560 feet, which is almost exactly twice the distance from [10] to [9] (2 x 282 = 564). This suggests a possible alignment with the TOL template if I place point [10] at the Scottish Rite HQ. The angle in the TOL between these two paths ([10]-[9] and [10]-[8]) is 40 degrees. The location of the Capital Building could meet this distance requirement yet still be at any angle other than 40 degrees. Is it at 40 degrees? Of course it is.

This is the first time in our investigation that I am using a scaled version of the TOL. Rather than using the exact form found on Oak Island, I am increasing its size so that the [10]-[9] path, which is normally 282 feet in length, is now 5x1152 feet in length. So, my new TOL is 20.4-ish times larger (5x1152/282 exactly). I am increasing it equally in all dimensions so as to preserve all ratios and all angles. This new TOL is almost 4.5 miles long and more than 2.75 miles wide.

With this newly sized (but identically scaled) Tree of Life, I place point [10] in the street (16th St) in front of Scottish Rite HQ. This street, if extended through Lafayette Square, bisects the White House, but the Scottish Rite HQ, obviously, does not sit in the middle of the road, so I cannot start atop the building. As with the White House Tree of Life, I orient this TOL to the south (180 degrees) from point [10]. The following alignments are noted (Figure 13). Point [9] is at the White House and point [8] is at the Capital Building (front steps), as expected. The path connecting points [9] and [8] overlays Pennsylvania Ave, which is to be expected. The path connecting points [7] and [8] runs the length of the Mall, centerline, and passes through the Washington Monument and Lincoln Memorial. Point [6] sits at the center of the Jefferson Memorial. The path connecting point [7] and the Knowledge point overlays the George Washington parkway. The path connecting points [7] and [1] passes through the middle of the traffic circle leading into Arlington Cemetery. The path connecting points [6] and [2] overlays the Memorial Bridge. The path connecting points [8] (Capital Bldg) and [1] passes down the middle of a runway at Washington National Airport and, if extended, passes through the front lawn of the George

Washington Masonic National Memorial. The runway alignment may be a coincidence, as I suspect the designers wanted that runway to face the Capital Building, but its alignment also with the GW MM grounds is odd. Most interestingly, if the path connecting points [7], [4], and [2] is extended to the south, it passes directly through point [10] on the GW MM TOL and through the Alexandria War Dead Monument (broken pillar) that is 114 feet further south. If this path is extended for another 284 miles to the south it will land you in Cedar Point, NC.

Although we used a scaled version of the TOL for this analysis, its dimensional ratios and angles were preserved. As such, while one can easily recognize patterns in the DC streets that form a pyramid, pentagram, compass/square, etc. (see Internet), a more subtle architecture is also in use, one that connects prominent features of Washington DC with the GW MM that lies just outside DC's original boundary, and with Cedar Point, NC further to the south. Given that the location of the White House and Capital Building have remained constant since L'Enfant's original DC plan in 1791, I think it is fair to conclude that he (or his approving authority George Washington) was aware of the pre-1795 Oak Island Tree of Life dimensions. Given that George Washington chose the location of Washington DC, and given its alignment with the Newport Tower and Oak Island, I conclude that Washington knew about these sites and their place in the larger American architecture, the Y shape that we have seen thus far. But, I am getting ahead of myself. I haven't yet shown the most interesting part. Our next stop is George Washington's location during his first inauguration and the initial planning of Washington DC: Manhattan.

But first, an honorable mention. Rhode Island Ave intersects Massachusetts Ave at 16th Street, north of the White House. Scott Circle marks this intersection. Rhode Island Ave travels eastward from Scott Circle at 66 degrees. Massachusetts Ave bears 114 degrees. Both of these angles differ from due east (90 degrees) by 24 degrees. Keep these numbers in mind (66, 2x57=114) as you read the next few chapters. They are the foundation of the map, once we bring all of this together. A few blocks further south, New York Ave departs the White House at 66 degrees. Now let's head there, to New York.

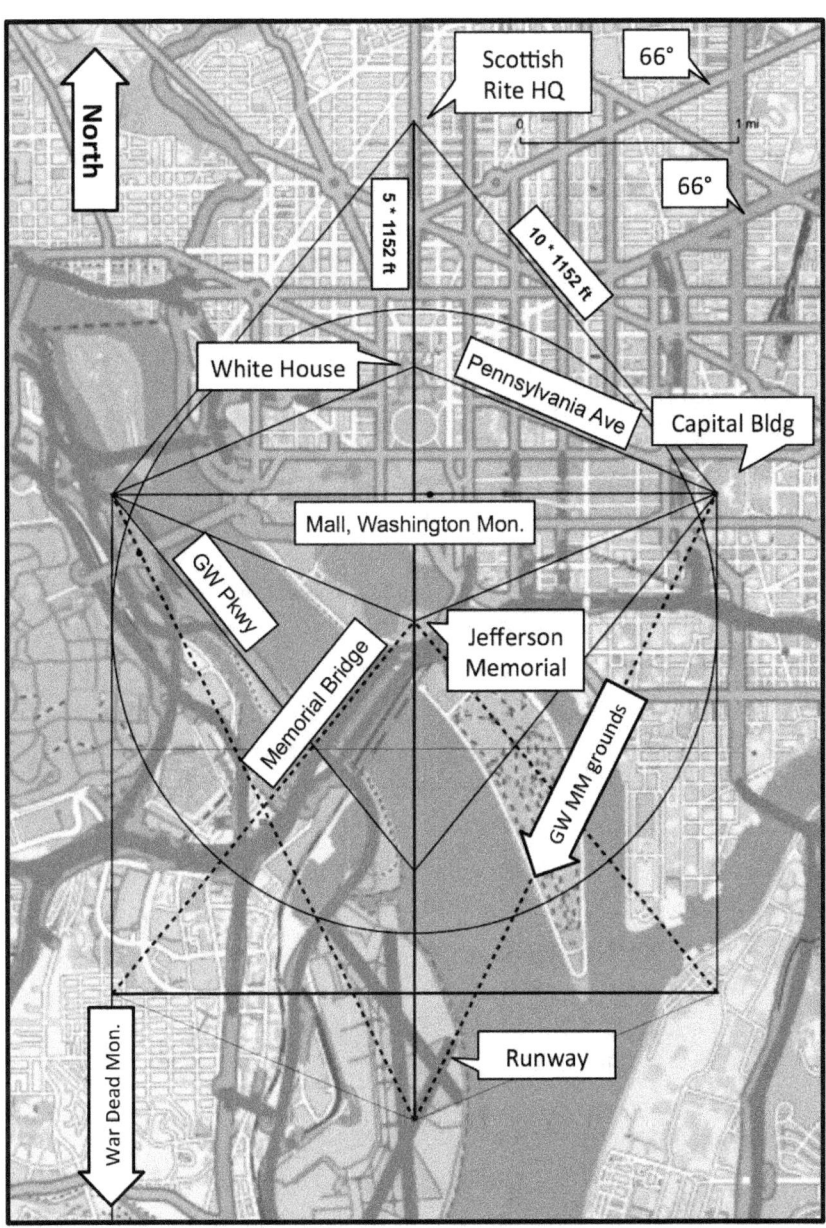

Figure 13: Washington DC with Tree of Life

The Center Column

If you were standing in front of the George Washington Masonic National Memorial facing its front door, you would be facing 279 degrees. If you turned clockwise 66 degrees you would be facing the same direction as the Alexandria War Dead Monument across the street (345 degrees). If you turned clockwise another 66 degrees you would be facing 51 degrees. If you traveled along that bearing for a few hundred miles you would run into the Statue of Liberty and a Tree of Life on Liberty Island.

Liberty Island, which is partially manmade, is nearly 1152 feet long and 720 feet wide, like the TOL (Figure 14). If the Knowledge point on the TOL is placed at the Liberty Island flagpole and the Tree of Life is oriented at 147 degrees from points [1] to [10], then the following matches exist between island features and the TOL template:

- Point [9], sometimes called Queen in the Qabalah, is beneath Lady Liberty.
- Point [6] is at the intersection of the two diagonal converging sidewalks.
- Point [3] is at the western right-angle corner of the island.
- Path [1]-[7] conforms to the northeastern edge of the island.
- Point [7] sits at the bend in the northeastern edge of the island.
- The azimuth of the Statue of Liberty TOL (147 degrees) is a key dimension of the TOL template, which has four segments 147 feet in

length. Make a mental note for later that 147 degrees is 33 degrees east of south (147 = 180 - 33). Liberty Island is 14.7 acres in size. Admittedly, this overlay is not awe-inspiring, but it will seem a better fit shortly. Regarding its Masonic origins, here is an excerpt from a Freemason website:[36]

Situated at the entrance of New York Harbor stands one of the most important symbols of American liberty... *The Statue of Liberty*. It was a gift from the French people to the United States as a token of mutual friendship. Its designer, a Freemason, was Brother Frederic A. Bartholdi (1834-1904) who conceived its design while on a visit to America. As his

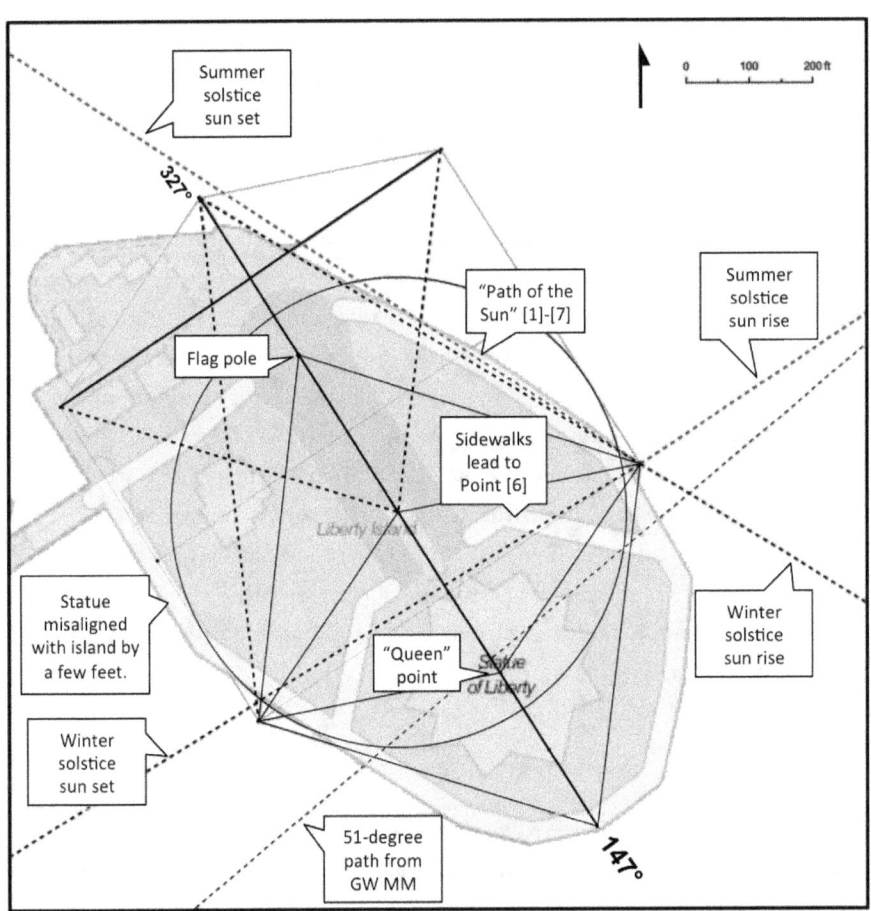

Figure 14: Liberty Island and its Tree of Life

---

[36] www.phoenixmasonry.org/masonicmuseum/statue_of_liberty.htm

ship sailed into New York, Bartholdi had a vision of a woman standing on a pedestal, holding a torch and welcoming immigrants to a new life in a free land. Along with Brother Bartholdi, Brother Gustave Eiffel was also responsible for the statue. Brother Eiffel designed and built the frame work which holds the copper sheeting in place.

They also include this story:

Frederic Bartholdi was one of the early members of Lodge Alsace-Lorraine, Paris (Oct. 14, 1875) which was composed of prominent intellectuals, writers and government representatives. When his famous statue 'Liberty Enlightening the World' was achieved, Bartholdi convened his Lodge to review it, even before the statue was shown to the U.S. committee. On June 19, 1884, the Lodge, **as if it were a pilgrimage**, went in a body to review his masterpiece. On July 4th, 1884 the finished statue was presented to the American Ambassador in Paris, Levi Morton. On August 5th, 1884, the then Grand Master of Masons in New York, William A. Brodie laid the cornerstone of the pedestal of the statue of 'Liberty Enlightening the World' with full Masonic ceremony.

The sunrise azimuth at the summer solstice and sunset azimuth at the winter solstice are one degree off the bearing of paths [2]-[3], [4]-[5], and [7]-[8]. The sunset azimuth at the summer solstice and sunrise azimuth at the winter solstice are one degree off the bearing of path [1]-[7], which is the northeastern edge of the island. Make a mental note for later of **path [1]-[7], which I call the Path of the Sun.** If the TOL shape were rotated one degree clockwise, paths [2]-[3], [4]-[5], and [7]-[8] and path [1]-[7] would align with the solstices, as seen at the Statue of Liberty. In other words, angles between paths on the TOL template match the angles between solstice rise and set lines at the latitude of the Statue of Liberty.

*****

If you were standing in front of the George Washington Masonic National Memorial facing its front door, you would be facing 279 degrees. If you turned clockwise 66 degrees you would be facing the same direction as the Alexandria War Dead Monument across the street (345 degrees). If you turned clockwise another 66 degrees you would be facing 51 degrees. If you traveled along that bearing for a few hundred miles you would pass right

through the Statue of Liberty and a Tree of Life on Liberty Island. If you
continued on this 51 degree path for another 2.4 miles you would reach an
obelisk in lower Manhattan, the Emmet obelisk, and another Tree of Life.

There are three well-known obelisks in Manhattan. I call them the three
pillars, as in the three pillars, or columns, of the Tree of Life. They are all
undeniably Masonic, they are all aligned with one another, and they are all
aligned with other things related to this investigation.

The northern-most obelisk, erected in 1881, is called Cleopatra's Needle.
It sits in Central Park within shouting distance of the New York Metropolitan
Museum of Art. It seems to have aged more in the 130 years that it has
endured the climate of New York City than it did in its 3500 years in the arid
Egyptian climate. The transport of this 70-foot, 224-ton granite object from
Egypt to New York City during 1877-1881 was a difficult feat of engineering
and logistics, especially given the technology at the time. Its ties to
Freemasonry are undeniable, as Freemasons led all aspects of the effort to
acquire, transport, and re-erect the obelisk. From the Wikipedia article on
Cleopatra's Needle:

> Jesse B. Anthony, Grand Master of Masons in the State of New York,
> presided as the cornerstone for the obelisk was laid in place with full
> Masonic ceremony on 2 October 1880. Over nine thousand Masons
> paraded up Fifth Avenue from 14th Street to 82nd Street and it was
> estimated that over fifty thousand spectators lined the parade route.[37]

The next obelisk, the Worth Monument, erected in 1857, is south of
Cleopatra's Needle. Beneath it lies the body of General William Jenkins
Worth (1794–1849). He was a prominent Freemason and war hero. Ft.
Worth, Texas and other places are named for him. But this is not a history
book, it's a book about numbers. The bearing from the Worth obelisk to
Cleopatra's Needle is 25.92 degrees.

The third obelisk, further to the south, was erected first, circa 1831,[38]
and is a monument to Thomas Addis Emmet,[39] a Freemason, NY State
Attorney General (1812-13), and Irishman of an especially rebellious nature.
The person is buried in Dublin, Ireland (after a brief stop at St. Mark's in

---

[37] http://en.wikipedia.org/wiki/Cleopatra's_Needle
[38] Allan Nevins, ed., The Diary of Philip Hone, 1828–1851 (NY: Dodd, Mead &
Company, 1927), Vol. 1, pp. 51–52, as seen at
http://www.nyu.edu/library/bobst/research/aia/logo.php
[39] http://en.wikipedia.org/wiki/Thomas_Addis_Emmet

New York City), and not in the cemetery at St. Paul's Chapel that holds the obelisk erected in his name. The monument seems to have its coordinates carved into it (40°42'40"N, 74°03'21"W), according to a St. Paul's Chapel guidebook from circa 2007.[40] I could make out the 3, 2, and 1 in my own photos, but the inscription is heavily worn and I was at a distance. The longitude is erroneous, as its actual longitude is 74°00'33.0" W, which is *exactly* 3-degrees east of the U.S. Capital Building's longitude.[41] The inscribed (erroneous) coordinates are in New Jersey, just beyond Liberty State Park, near Liberty Island. I suspect that the erroneous coordinates, conspicuously marked with sequential numbers 3-2-1, are meant to draw attention to the real coordinate (33.0 arc-seconds). The numbers 3-2-1 can be rewritten as 32+1 = 33. As we will see shortly, the number 33 is very important at this location. I also note that the opposite direction of 321 degrees is 141 degrees (321-180=141), which is half the length of the 282-foot segments in the Oak Island Tree of Life. For example, the distance on the TOL from the buried stone to the Knowledge point is 141 feet. Also, the Emmet obelisk faces 123 degrees, which is 321 written backwards. The opposite of 123 degrees is 303 degrees (303=123+180), and **303** draws attention to 33. Anyway, the bearing from the Emmet obelisk to the Worth obelisk is 25.94 degrees. The bearing from the Emmet obelisk to Cleopatra's Needle is 25.93 degrees. So, the bearings between all three of the obelisks (25.92, 25.94, 25.93) differ by no more than two one-hundredths of a degree, which is a perfect alignment. For simplicity, we can round up and say that the obelisks form a line bearing 26 degrees.

A 26-degree rhumb line from the Emmet obelisk (southern most) to Cleopatra's Needle (northern most) passes through the following:

- Washington Square (through the statue of Garibaldi, a Grand Master Mason and Italian revolutionary[42]),
- The New York Public Library main branch building,
- The Empire State Building (on 33rd St.).

If this line is extended to the south it passes through the exact center of the old U.S. Customs House, now a Smithsonian museum. Specifically, the line

---

[40] http://forgotten-ny.com/2007/09/mystery-of-the-obelisks-guest-page-by-martin-langfield-author-of-the-malice-box/

[41] The coordinates of the U.S. Capital Building are (38°53'23.29"N, 77°00'33"W), which means that the U.S. Capital Building is exactly 3-degrees west of the Emmet obelisk (and further south, of course).

[42] http://www.masonicdictionary.com/garibaldi.html

passes through a statue in front of the building of a stoic woman in Egyptian attire holding a flower (on the left to someone facing the building).[43]

As revealed above, a rhumb line from the George Washington Masonic National Memorial in Alexandria, Virginia to the Emmet obelisk (southern most) passes through the Statue of Liberty (through Lady Liberty herself, not merely the island) along a bearing of 51.06 degrees. In other words, the GW MM, Statue of Liberty, and Emmet obelisk are aligned (see book cover).

A rhumb line from point [6] to point [4] on the Liberty Island TOL (Figure 14), if extended to the north, bisects the New York Metropolitan Museum of Art, behind which sits Cleopatra's Needle. I consider this one to be a meaningless coincidence.

It might not be a coincidence, though, that path [6]-[4] on our Liberty Island TOL, if extended northward, passes through, or within a few feet of the statue of Shakespeare in Central Park. This statue sits on the eastern side of a circular pathway that surrounds a circular flower bed. This circle is at the southern end of a long straight walkway in Central Park called The Mall. On the opposite side of the circular pathway is a statue of Columbus. The statue of Columbus faces Shakespeare, and vice versa. We have encountered Columbus a few times during this investigation, such as the word Columbia in Washington DC. Columbus, in a way, was a symbol for the United States itself (the New World): "The federal district was named Columbia, which was a poetic name for the United States commonly in use at that time [1790]."[44] Columbus Ave. in Sandusky intersects Washington St. at the heart of Washington Park and a Tree of Life oriented at 66 degrees. The angle 66, which is also a length dimension of the Tree of Life template (Figure 2), will come up several more times. Back in Central Park, if 66th Street were extended through the park it would pass over the dueling statues of Columbus and Shakespeare.

The three obelisks mentioned above, our three pillars, are not the only obelisks in Manhattan. It's a three-dimensional landscape. I conducted a one-day exhausting, but not exhaustive, survey of lower Manhattan during an expensive jaunt into the city. I paid $20 for a pastrami sandwich, all for you, the reader. A few blocks from the Central Park statues, at the corner of 57th St. and Park Ave., is the Ritz Tower. The tower is capped by an obelisk and a

---

[43] http://en.wikipedia.org/wiki/Alexander_Hamilton_U.S._Custom_House#/media/File:AHCH-1Asia_jeh.JPG

[44] http://en.wikipedia.org/wiki/Washington,_D.C.

pyramid, which itself is cornered by four smaller obelisks. A plaque on the
building notes that the "tower [is] capped by obelisks and a pyramidal roof."
A line drawn from point [1] on the Liberty Island Tree of Life through the
Worth obelisk intersects the corner of this building. That's odd, but I cannot
find a reason to consider it important. I'll plant a seed now that the number
57 (as in 57th street) will be an important dimension in the multi-state shape
that we are building (hint: 90, 33, 57 are interior angles of a right triangle).

Further south, after I completed my hurried exploration of Liberty
Island, I noticed a building with several obelisks on it near the old U.S.
Customs House at the southern tip of Manhattan. If one draws a line from
the center of this building bearing 26 degrees it will pass through our three
pillars: the Emmet, Worth, and Egyptian obelisks. In other words, it is on our
26-degree line. I did not see a name on this building, but its address was
clearly marked in several places, including an engraving on the facade of the
building: 26 Broadway (see Figure 15). An Internet search revealed that this
building was originally known as the Standard Oil building, which was
extensively remodeled and expanded during 1921-28. If you consider its
address (26 Broadway) to be a coincidental match with its 26 degree
alignment with the three Masonic obelisks, consider the visitor brochure at
the George Washington Masonic National Memorial that notes that the GW
MM "is capped with a pyramid and surmounted by a stylized finial,
symbolizing Light," and that "The [GW] Memorial is a *beacon* that spreads the
Light of Freemasonry... to the world."[45] Compare those words with the
Wikipedia description of 26 Broadway, which notes that it "is topped by a
pyramid" [between the four obelisks] and that "at the time of completion, the
pyramid was the tallest tower at the southern tip of Manhattan and was
illuminated as a *beacon* for ships entering the harbor."[46] Manhattan was
already a well-lit place at the time (1928). The 26 Broadway pyramid is
modeled after the Mausoleum at Halicarnassus,[47] one of the seven wonders of
the ancient world. If you doubt 26 Broadway's connection with Freemasonry,
consider the visitor webpage[48] of the Scottish Rite HQ in Washington DC,
which reads: "The House of the Temple is located at 1733 Sixteenth Street,[49]

---

[45] Why is the word light capitalized, as if a formal name?

[46] http://en.wikipedia.org/wiki/26_Broadway

[47] http://en.wikipedia.org/wiki/Mausoleum_at_Halicarnassus

[48] http://scottishrite.org/headquarters/visitors/

[49] 17+16=33, so 1733, 16th St = 33+33 = 66

NW, in the District of Columbia... [and] has served as the national headquarters of the Supreme Council since 1915.... Its architecture is an adaptation of the famous Mausoleum at Halicarnassus, one of the 'Seven Wonders of the Ancient World.'" Both 26 Broadway and the Ritz Tower were designed (or co-designed) by architect Thomas Hastings, who also designed the New York Public Library main branch, which is bisected by our 26-degree rhumb line, as noted above. The Library sports 52-foot ceilings (52=2x26). Here we have a consistent architectural theme of pyramids (one style in particular), obelisks, and beacons, along with precise geographic alignments emphasizing the numbers 26 and 66 (two sixes). Some of these buildings are overt Masonic structures, such as Scottish Rite HQ and the GW MM, and some are corporate skyscrapers (gigantic obelisks). Other American buildings fit this theme, such as Los Angeles City Hall (and Public Library), Chicago's Metropolitan Tower,[50] and Cincinnati's PNC Tower,[51] all of which that have silly explanations for their odd architecture and beacons, e.g., Metropolitan Tower: "The pyramid symbolized longevity and permanence and the beehive stood for industry and thrift. When first installed, the beehive also contained four directional beacons, a metaphor for the company's global reach." Nonsense. Even the odd symbol of the beehive is Masonic, as it is present on a Mason's apron and in Masonic artwork. Cincinnati's PNC Tower (1913) was designed by Cass Gilbert, the same architect that designed the Woolworth Building in Manhattan at 233 Broadway, which is two blocks north of the Emmet obelisk and is split by our 26-degree line. Did you notice the address—233 Broadway—and that adding the 3s gives you 26 Broadway (or is it 2x33=66; perhaps both)? Another Gilbert building, designed in 1926, is the New York Life building (51 Madison Ave), which is topped by a gold (light) pyramid. This building rises 1000 feet due east of the Worth obelisk and sits on 26th Street. Yes, Gilbert was a Freemason.[52] By the way, the pyramid-shaped Mausoleum at Halicarnassus

---

[50] http://en.wikipedia.org/wiki/Metropolitan_Tower_(Chicago)
The Metropolitan Tower is listed at 145 meters in height. I am going to guess that it is actually 147 meters in height (the height of the Great Pyramid at Giza).
[51] http://en.wikipedia.org/wiki/PNC_Tower
The PNC Tower is 151 meters tall to the top of its beacon. I am going to guess that it is 147 meters to the top of the pyramid (the height of the Great Pyramid at Giza).
[52] http://www.ofmasoniclodge.org/?_escaped_fragment_=masonic-art19/zoom/ch1r/image1ebt#!masonic-art19/zoom/ch1r/image1ebt

was 147 feet tall, a key dimension in the TOL template (Figure 2) and the bearing of the Liberty Island TOL.[53]

To make things more confusing, Chicago's Metropolitan Tower is one block from the eastern end of Historic Route 66.[54] Here's an odd claim from the Internet: "The famous old American highway 'Route 66' was laid out by Freemasons with the apparent intention of sending masses of automobile riders into a self-processing occult 'trip.'"[55] I doubt that. I only mention this Internet claim because enough Freemasons clearly feel a tie to Route 66, as if it's an inside joke, to justify the selling of coffee mugs, ties, and other items featuring the Route 66 emblem overlaid by the Masonic Compass and Square. Which of these "patterns" are noise and which are clues? Did you notice the New York Life address: 51 MAdiSON Ave. Mason Ave. DI is **501** in Roman numerals; this is the bearing from the GW MM to the Emmet Obelisk. I have no reason to believe that this is intentional, but it's fun to see. Do not worry: a consistent narrative is emerging that will help us decide which clues belong on the map.

Regarding the 26-degree line, is it only a coincidence that Theodore Roosevelt, a prominent Freemason, was the 26th President of the United States? Yes, actually, that one is only a coincidence. Or is it?! Yes. But it is fun to also note that FDR, the 32nd President, was a 32-degree Scottish Rite Freemason, and the 33rd President, Truman, was a 33-degree Scottish Rite Freemason. All future presidents cannot be Freemasons because the degrees stop at 33. The buck stopped with Truman. Anyway...

What is the meaning of the obelisks and the 26-degree line? Only the architects know the meaning of their symbols. But I'll take a guess. The three pillars of Freemasonry represent to Masons a Trinity of Wisdom, Strength, and Balance. Other words are sometimes used, but they all mean the same three things pertaining to the three columns of the Qabalah Tree of Life. The three obelisks of Manhattan each have a quality that might correlate them with this Trinity. General Worth is Strength. Emmet, the Attorney General, is Balance (the balanced scales of Justice), and Cleopatra's Needle (which has nothing to do with Cleopatra herself) is the Wisdom of the ages.

---

[53] http://www.softschools.com/facts/wonders_of_the_world/ mausoleum_at_halicarnassus_facts/70/

[54] http://en.wikipedia.org/wiki/U.S._Route_66

[55] http://vigilantcitizen.com/vigilantreport/ top-10-most-sinister-psyops-mission-patches/

Or, perhaps Emmet, a recognized scholar, represents Wisdom, and Cleopatra represents Balance through female leadership. Regardless, I suspect that the traits of the three obelisks represent the three pillars of the Tree of Life and aim to suggest the TOL to be a key to the puzzle. But how should that key be applied? Hall notes that 26 is the Hebrew numeric value for the name of God:

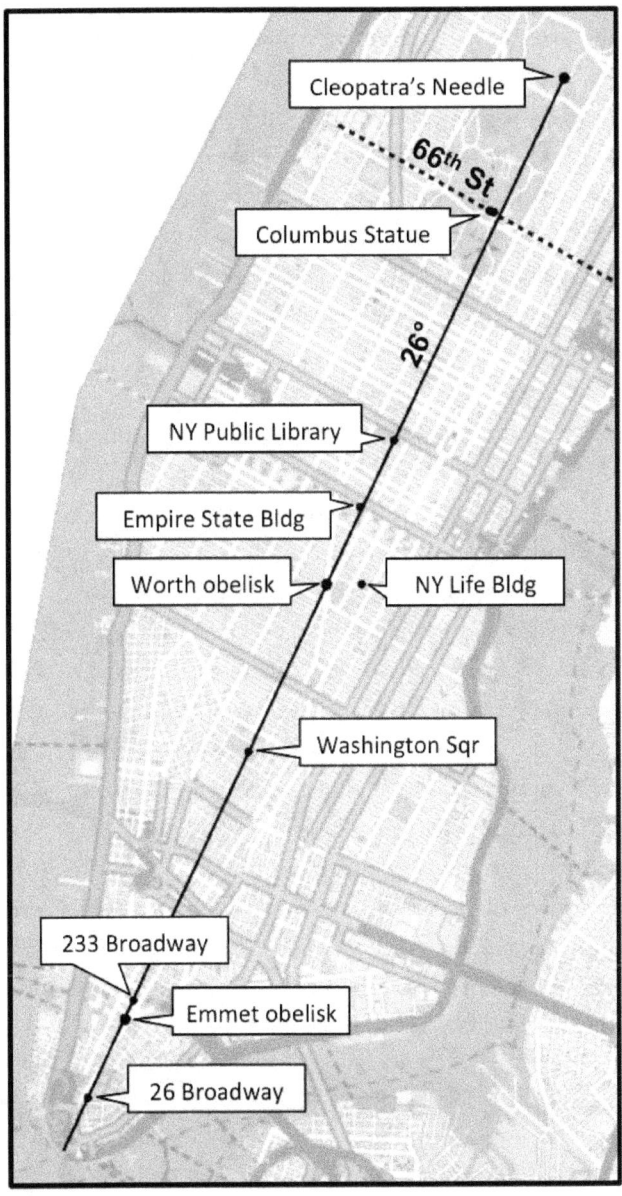

Figure 15: Manhattan obelisks and the 26-degree path

The Demiurgus of the Jews is called in English Jehovah, but when seeking the numerical value of the name Jehovah it is necessary to resolve the name into its Hebrew letters... The Hebrew letters are: [He, Vau, He, Yod], and when reversed into the English order from left to right read: Yod-He-Vau-He [Jehovah]. By [assigning each Hebrew letter its numeric value], it is found that the four characters of this sacred name have the following numerical significance: Yod equals 10. He equals 5, Vau equals 6, and the second He equals 5. Therefore, 10+5+6+5=26, a synonym of Jehovah.

Most importantly, the 26-degree line in Manhattan might be a clue to the means by which we started this quest: we followed the center column of the Oak Island Tree of Life to the Newport Tower. Also, as we will soon see, the center column of the Trees of Life that we have uncovered, and the ones that we will uncover, are the primary keys to assembling and *deciphering* our map. Hall, during his description of the Qabalah and the Tree of Life, explains that 26 is the number for the center column of the TOL, as determined by adding its Sephiroth (points):

Three vertical columns support the universal system as typified by the Sephirothic Tree [of Life]. The central pillar has its foundation in Kether [point 1], the Eternal One. It passes downward through the hypothetical Sephira, Daath [Knowledge point], and then through Tiphereth [point 6] and Jesod [point 9], with its lower end resting upon the firm foundation of Malchuth [point 10], the last of the globes. The true import of the central pillar is equilibrium. It demonstrates how the Deity always manifests by emanating poles of expression from the midst of Itself but remaining free from the illusion of polarity [Meaning: the Deity is not Good or Evil, but both *and* neither]. If the numbers of the four Sephiroth connected by this column be added together (1+6+9+10), the sum is 26, the number of Jehovah.

The 26-degree obelisk line is telling us to pay close attention to the center column of the Tree of Life, which we used to point us from Oak Island to the Newport Tower. Let's heed this call and make a mental note of the Liberty Island TOL center column, which bears 147 degrees.

The Church and its Spire

I won't lie to you and pretend that my next move came from some deeply intellectual discovery, as you've likely come to expect from me. The mega-hit movie *National Treasure*, starring a gorgeous German actress and some other people, pursued a Freemason treasure of ridiculous proportions until its discovery deep beneath Trinity Church in Manhattan's Financial District.[56] The Emmet obelisk at St. Paul's Chapel is a few blocks north of Trinity Church. So, while contemplating deeply intellectual things (and German actresses), I used Google Earth to measure the distance between the Emmet obelisk and parts of Trinity Church and its cemetery. In the northeastern corner (the Masonic cornerstone) of the Trinity Church cemetery is a highly conspicuous monument, a large spire memorializing prisoners of the American Revolutionary War. A sign on it reads: "Soldier's Monument / Designed by Frank Wills / 1852." One of its inscriptions reads, in part, that it is dedicated to "those great and good Men who died whilst in Captivity in the old Sugar House and were interred in Trinity Church Yard." It is 1152 feet from the Emmet obelisk, which bears 33.0 degrees from the spire. Placing point [10] of the unscaled Tree of Life template (1152-by-720

---

[56] In the movie's narrative, the main character is admonished for *wasting his life* chasing a series of seemingly unresolvable clues until he discovers the *true* treasure of Freemasonry *hidden beneath* the Church.

feet) at the Emmet obelisk and orienting it at 33.0 and 213.0 degrees, places point [1] on the Revolutionary War spire. The remainder of the points on the TOL seem unremarkable in their location (as Manhattan now looks). At second glance, one notices that point [2] sits almost on 120 Cedar St and point [3] sits where 72 Cedar St. would be if it existed. Recall that the angle between the paths from our three points at Cedar Point, OH, Cedar Point, NC, and the Newport Tower to the GW MM is 120 degrees. The dimensions of our TOL are 16x72 feet (1152 ft) and 10x72 feet (720 ft). Also, 72 degrees is an interior angle of a pentagram, an important 5-by-8 ratio Masonic symbol (like our TOL). What marks this as a Tree of Life is Cedar St., which cuts above the [2]-[3] path of this TOL. It is also cut by Liberty St and Maiden Ln (remember the Virgin [Maiden] of the Third Degree). Trinity Church sits adjacent to 72 Trinity Place, if that address existed. The spire is adjacent to a large building at 111 Broadway. The 111 could be viewed to represent our three pillars, but it's probably just a number. Given that none of the other points match nearby landmarks, perhaps this one should be called a Center Column of Life. But there is little chance that it is a coincidence given its precise 33-degree orientation and 1152 foot distance. Note for later the alignment between path [1]-[8] and the summer solstice sunrise and winter solstice sunset. Another Path of the Sun.

The distance from the Soldier's Monument spire to the center of 26 Broadway is 1152 ft (the length of our TOL). The center of the building is not the center of its pyramid, since the pyramid sits atop a tower that is the southern half of the building. So, our 1152-foot line ends at the northern wall of this tower. The angle from this point to the spire is 19 degrees. This gives us 19 degrees from 26 Broadway to the spire, 26 degrees from 26 Broadway to the Emmet obelisk (and other obelisks), and 33 degrees from the spire to the Emmet obelisk. The difference between all of these angles is 7 degrees. I can only speculate an explanation for this. Perhaps it means nothing, although a quick read of any religious, spiritual, mythological, or other such text will reveal that seven is considered a sacred number: 7 days of the week, 7 horsemen of the apocalypse, 7 seas, 7 wonders of the ancient world, etc. Freemasons also talk of seven as the combination of three (a triangle) and four (a square), each with their own symbolic meanings. Together, these two shapes form a square-based pyramid, as sits in Egypt and atop all of these Masonic buildings that we are encountering. Last, these three points (the spire, 26 Broadway, and the Emmet obelisk) form a triangle with interior angles of 7, 7, and 166 degrees. I couldn't pass on an opportunity to mention a number with 66 in it.

Cedar St. marks the placement of a TOL here, but we will find that the number 33 is the cryptic purpose of this otherwise unremarkable TOL. Figure 16 is the final piece of our puzzle. None of those pieces have been particularly remarkable on their own. When combined, though, a single coherent theme emerges. Let's assemble the map.

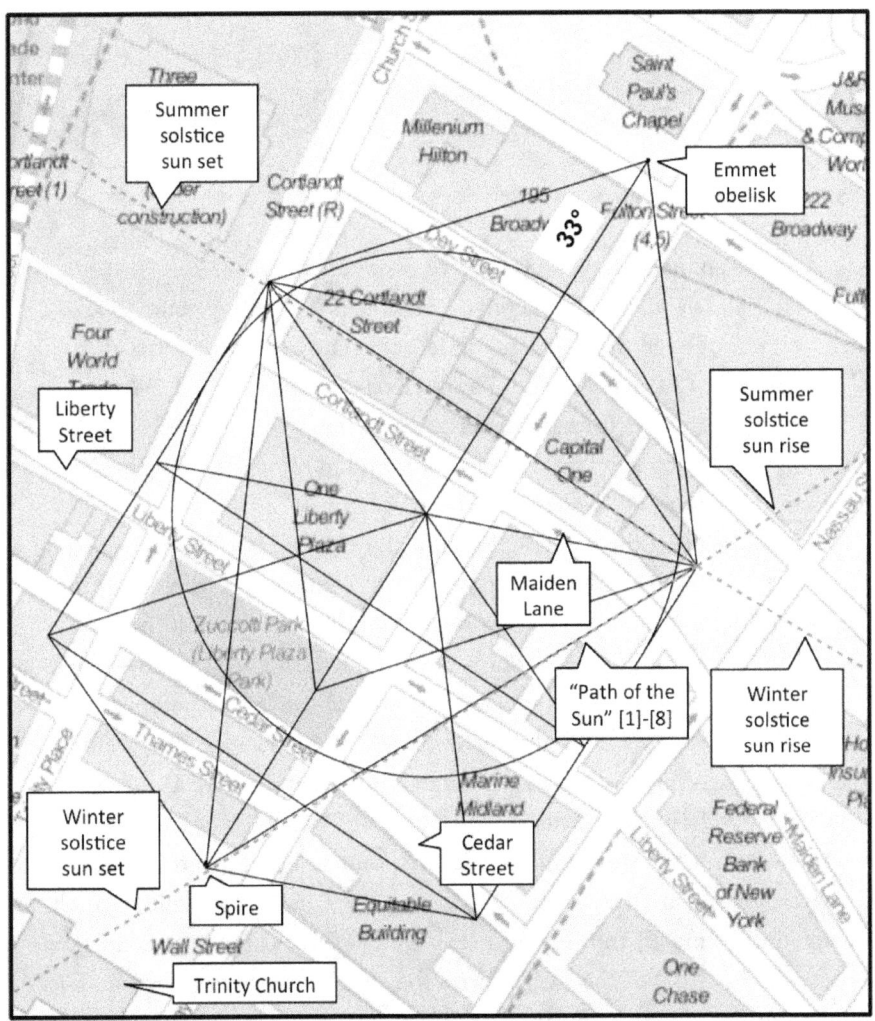

Figure 16: Trinity Church and its Tree of Life

The Cedar Points

Here is an inventory of what we've uncovered thus far.

On Oak Island, a place synonymous since 1795 with treasure, is an arrangement of large stones, some buried, that can be interpreted as forming a Qabalah Tree of Life (Figure 2). The Tree of Life template is 1152 feet long, 720 feet wide, and has four segments along its length of 147 feet. If a circle with a radius of 360 feet is centered at point [6] in this TOL, it creates segments along the TOL's length of 66 and 213 feet (213 = 147+66).

If we trust that the center column of the Oak Island TOL points along a bearing of 239.54 degrees, then it points along a rhumb line directly at the Newport Tower, roughly 412 miles away. This line also passes through central Washington DC and a south-facing Tree of Life (Figure 13). The sunset azimuth on the winter solstice at the Newport Tower points along a rhumb line that passes through Washington DC and through the grounds of the George Washington Masonic National Memorial (GW MM).

The Oak Island TOL shape, if oriented at 279 and 99 degrees, overlays features on the GW MM grounds at every point along its length. The winter solstice sunset azimuth from the Newport Tower aligns well with the path connecting points [6] and [3] on the GW MM TOL. Other alignments are observed. Point [7] of the TOL sits on the start of Cedar St. According to the Freemason publication *Morals and Dogma*, a branch of acacia [cedar] "represents" the Tree of Life. The Alexandria War Dead Monument, which is directly south of point [10] of the GW MM TOL, is 1152 feet from the southwest corner of the GW MM fence and is aligned with the south side of that fence. This monument was allegedly created from a broken pillar originally intended for the GW MM. The War Dead Monument faces 345 degrees, which is 66 degrees north of the GW MM azimuth (279 degrees).

The sunset azimuth on the summer solstice at the GW MM creates a path along a rhumb line to Washington Park in Sandusky, Ohio at nearly the same distance as from the Newport Tower to the GW MM. A TOL oriented at 66 degrees matches several features in the park and aligns perfectly with Washington St, also bearing 66 degrees from north. The park is centered at the intersection of Washington St and Columbus Ave, which could be interpreted as the intersection of Washington and Columbia, as in "Washington DC." The park contains a Masonic emblem display and is across the street from Sandusky's Masonic Lodge. The original street plan for downtown Sandusky was designed by Sandusky's first Master Mason to reflect the Compass and Square of Freemasonry. This Master Mason's father was a United States Surveyor of Public Lands. Branching off of downtown Sandusky is Cedar Point, which is due west of the Newport Tower.

Due south of the GW MM is Cedar Point, NC, which began as a 2080 acre plot granted in 1713 to Thomas Lee, a prominent figure in Northern Virginia. Cedar Point, NC is home to a Masonic Campus.

A scaled TOL template, when placed at the Scottish Rite HQ in Washington DC overlays numerous features in DC, including the White House, Capital building, and Jefferson Memorial. The TOL's western column points through point [10] of the GW MM TOL, the Alexandria War Dead Monument, and Cedar Point, NC. A TOL alignment is also observed around the White House grounds. The White House has 147 windows.

The Oak Island Tree of Life template matches several features of Liberty Island, if oriented at 147 and 327 degrees, and matches the length and width of the 14.7 acre island.

The Oak Island Tree of Life vaguely matches a few features around Trinity Church, particularly when connected with the Emmet obelisk at St. Paul's Chapel and oriented at 33 and 213 degrees. Erroneous coordinates on the Emmet obelisk seem to draw attention to the number 33, which is the bearing of Broadway in this part of Manhattan. Cedar St. marks this TOL, which also crosses Liberty St. and Maiden Ln.

Now, let us put it all together.

*****

The Inverted Triangle of the 33rd Degree. Cedar Point, OH bears 327 degrees from Cedar Point, NC, or *147* degrees in the opposite direction. Note that 327 degrees is 33 degrees west of north (360-33 = 327), and 147 degrees is 33 degrees east of south. This orientation is identical to the orientation of the Liberty Island Tree of Life.

The Newport Tower bears 33.7 degrees from Cedar Point, NC. This is a near-mirror of the path from Cedar Point, NC to Cedar Point, OH. It is also almost identical to the 33.0-degree orientation of the Trinity Church TOL. But why the 0.7 degree error? Did the architects get sloppy? I estimate that Colonial-era mapping technology could achieve about a half-degree of precision at these large scales. What do we find if we adjust our bearing from Cedar Point, NC to something closer to 33.0 degrees than 33.7 degrees? What else but Cedar Point, Rhode Island (41.404704, -71.493410).

Like Cedar Point, OH, Cedar Point, RI is not a town; it is a north-pointed peninsula. It is southwest of the Newport Tower and across the bay. It is labeled on Google Maps and Google Earth as "Cedar Point." It is in or near the township of Narraganset, RI and looks to me like private property. We now have a triangle formed of three Cedar Points, with one side mimicking the Liberty Island TOL and another side mimicking the Trinity Church TOL (see Figure 17).

Please recall that I have been operating on a loan from the reader since we began this journey to permit me to rotate the Oak Island TOL by 0.24 degrees from the orientation of Amundsen's GPS coordinates, which I suspected of having inaccuracies. In retrospect, was my decision correct? If one draws a rhumb line along my adjusted Oak Island TOL bearing (239.54 degrees) from Oak Island to the Newport Tower, 412 miles away, and extends that line a few miles across the bay, it passes through a north-pointed peninsula called Cedar Point. My realignment worked, as the Oak Island TOL (center column) points to both the Newport Tower and Cedar Point, RI. Take that a step further. If we continue the rhumb line that passes down the Oak Island TOL center column and through the Newport Tower and Cedar Point, RI, we eventually pass through the start of Cedar Point Rd, which is the entrance to Cedar Point County Park on Long Island (41.028022,

-72.225605). This line eventually passes through Washington DC. Loan repaid in full.

From the perspective of someone at Cedar Point, NC, the angle between the lines to Cedar Point, RI (+33) and Cedar Point, OH (-33) is 66 degrees, which is the orientation of the Sandusky (Washington Park) TOL and is a dimension of the TOL template. So, each of these three Trees of Life—Liberty Island (147 degrees), Trinity Church (33 degrees), and Washington Park in Sandusky (66 degrees)—are oriented in a manner that reveals a key dimension of the triangle formed by connecting the three Cedar Points (NC, OH, and RI). All of these angles are also segment lengths in the TOL template (Figure 2).

To summarize, there are three Cedar Points that form a triangle with angles between its sides of 66 (2x33), 57, and 57 degrees. The Liberty Island TOL reflects the path from Cedar Point, OH to Cedar Point, NC (147 degrees). The Trinity Church TOL reflects the path from Cedar Point, NC to Cedar Point, RI (33 degrees). The White House TOL or Scottish Rite HQ TOL reflects the path from the GW MM to Cedar Point, NC (180 degrees).

What does the GW MM TOL reflect? Frankly, I don't know. But its

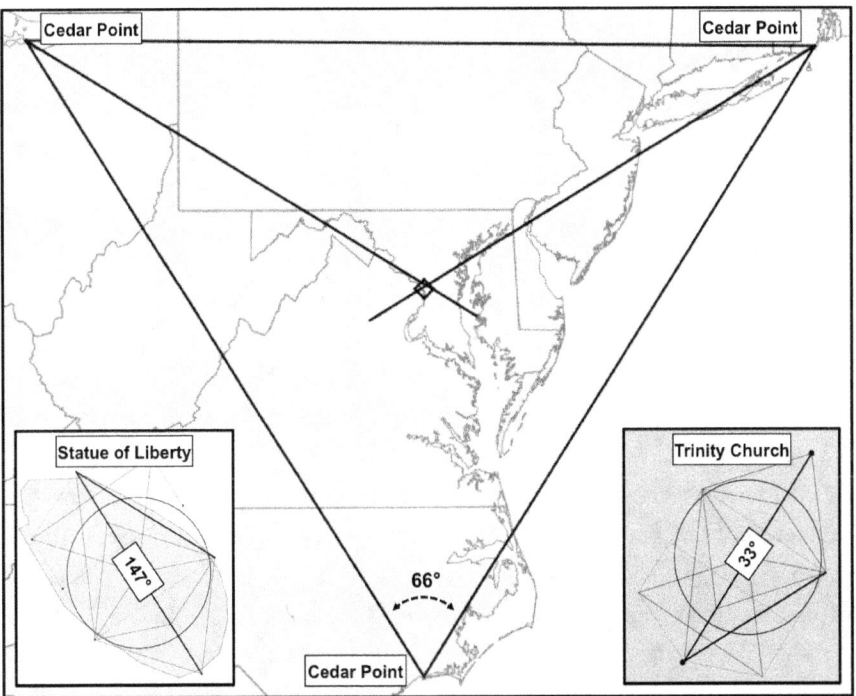

Figure 17: Inverted Triangle of the 33rd Degree with Paths of the Sun

orientation fits the mathematical pattern of the New York Trees of Life.
Here is how. If one starts at Cedar Point, OH and heads toward Cedar Point,
NC they will do so along a bearing of 147 degrees. To shift from this path to
the next path, which is from Cedar Point, NC to Cedar Point, RI, one must
follow these steps: add 66 degrees, then flip 180 degrees. So, 147 degrees plus
66 degrees puts us on 213 degrees. Flip 180 degrees and we are headed to RI
at 33 degrees. Bingo. Now, do that again: 33 degrees plus 66 degrees puts us
on 99 degrees. Flip 180 degrees and we are headed at 279 degrees. What
TOL has an orientation of 99 and 279 degrees? The George Washington
Masonic National Memorial Tree of Life. If you do that again (279+66-180),
then you face 165 degrees and are headed in the southerly direction of Russell
Rd in Alexandria, VA, as it heads toward the Alexandria War Dead
Monument. Do it again (165+66-180) and you are facing 51 degrees, the
direction from the GW MM to the Statue of Liberty and Emmet obelisk.
Along this path of 51 degrees, three Trees of Life are aligned: GW MM,
Liberty Island, and Trinity Church.

It's probably just a coincidence, but 165 equals 5x33, which is the
intersection at a corner of the Empire State Bldg (5th and 33rd streets).
Similarly, many of the angles that we've encountered contain multiples of 33.

66 = 2 x 33

99 = 3 x 33

165 = 5 x 33

147 = 180 - 1 x 33

213 = 180 + 1 x 33

279 = 180 + 3 x 33

345 = 180 + 5 x 33

There are clues to this shape throughout our investigation. Washington
St in Sandusky bears 66 degrees. 66th St passes over the Columbus and
Shakespeare statues in Central Park. The War Dead Monument in Alexandria
faces 345 degrees, which is 66 degrees north of 279 degrees, the orientation of
King St and the GW MM. The Trinity Church TOL points to the south at
213 degrees, which is 66 degrees south of 279 degrees, the GW MM
orientation. The Statue of Liberty and Emmet obelisk bear 51 degrees from
the GW MM, which is 66 degrees clockwise from the Alexandria War Dead
Monument (345 degrees). The Woolworth Building is 233 Broadway
(2x33=66). But here's one that I haven't mentioned already...

Old Beach Road, the road heading east from Touro Park, which is home to the Newport Tower, bears 66 degrees. On the corner of Old Beach Rd, in the lot diagonal Touro Park, is the Redwood Library, designed by a noted Freemason. The crossed sidewalks between the library and the street (Old Beach Rd) are not aligned with Old Beach Rd. The sidewalks mimic the orientation of the Alexandria War Dead Monument—the sidewalk leading from Old Beach Rd to the building bears 345 degrees. At the end of that sidewalk, against the building, is a statue of George Washington resting his coat on a broken pillar. This statue bears 66 degrees from the Newport Tower and is 147 meters away (the height of the Great Pyramid at Giza).[57]

In this mess of numbers, I wonder if I'm beginning to see shadows. Heading west from Washington DC is Interstate 66. Did you notice in Figure 7 that King St is also known as Route 7, which passes over point [7] on the Tree of Life at the GW MM (modeled after two of the seven wonders of the ancient world: Lighthouse at Alexandria and Mausoleum at Halicarnassus)? The grid-pattern streets of Washington DC are bordered on the east and the west (in its central grid) by 26th Street. Which numbers are coincidence and which are cryptic signs deliberately placed?

Our favorite number 66, represents, in part, balance: 33 to the left and 33 to the right. The prolific use of 33 degrees implicates Scottish Rite Freemasonry in this plan, with high confidence. The prolific use of 147 also points a finger at someone specific. Here comes our first clue as to whom.

*****

We have one more feature to add to our inverted triangle made of Cedar Points. On the Tree of Life template two paths point 26.5 degrees[58] from the center column: path [1]-[7] and path [1]-[8]; they form the arms of the Masonic Compass on my rendering of the TOL (Figure 2). At the Liberty Island TOL, the winter solstice sunrise and summer solstice sunset azimuths align with path [1]-[7]. At the Trinity Church TOL in Manhattan, the winter solstice sunset and summer solstice sunrise azimuths align with path [1]-[8]. When I introduced the Liberty Island TOL earlier in this book I called this path the "path of the sun," for lack of a more clever name. When I first

---

[57] The Great Pyramid at Giza is 147 meters in height (to its nonexistent peak). http://en.wikipedia.org/wiki/Great_Pyramid_of_Giza

[58] ArcTan[360/723]*180/Pi

observed these alignments, it *felt* to me unlikely that they were a coincidence, given the Compass's symbolic connection to the divine (it descends downward), and the sun's connection to divine light.

A moment ago, I noted that the Liberty Island TOL has the same 147-degree orientation as the path from Cedar Point, Ohio to Cedar Point, North Carolina. I also noted that the Trinity Church TOL has the same 33-degree orientation as the Cedar Point, Rhode Island to Cedar Point, NC path. So, let's pretend that the paths from Cedar Point, NC to Cedar Point, RI and Cedar Point, OH form the center columns of two giant Trees of Life, both with point [10] at Cedar Point, NC. Let's then plot the "path of the sun" for each of these Trees of Life. This approach creates a line from Cedar Point, RI that bears 239.7[59] degrees and a line from Cedar Point, OH that bears 120.4 degrees. Do these bearings (120, 240) look familiar? They should. They are the sunrise and sunset azimuths that led us from the Newport Tower to the GW MM to Sandusky, OH (rounded off). At these bearings (239.7, 120.4) the two lines intersect each other within the current Washington DC boundary, north of the U.S. Capital building.

We now have a map that includes an inverted triangle, centered at the GW MM, with two sun paths (light) that cross the triangle and intersect inside the square of Washington DC (see Figure 17). This crossed-triangle shape has important meaning within the *Sacred Mysteries* (e.g., Freemasonry), which will be revealed when we decipher the map.

*****

The Divine Trinity. The Statue of Liberty is actually named "Liberty Enlightening the World." Lady Liberty is a personification of enlightenment, or that which enlightens. The word *enlightens* suggests reasoned intellectual ambitions. Light symbolizes that intellectual ascension, the discovery of Truth, which in Freemasonry is "represented by Light," according to Pike and others. The architectural design of the base of the Statue of Liberty is identical to each of the three levels of the tower of the George Washington Masonic National Memorial. It displays four pillars, each bordering a vertical window (creating three windows), in a four-sided stone shape. Four pillars plus three windows equals seven. Four represents the Earth, as in the four compass directions and the four seasons. Three represents the Deity

---

[59] 239.67 degrees. Compare with the Oak Island TOL azimuth (239.54 degrees).

(Trinity). Together they make the sacred number seven. The pyramid is an Earth-bound square (4) topped by ascending triangles (3), and is the perfect representation of the connection between the Earth and the Deity, according to the symbolism of the *Sacred Mysteries*.

According to its visitor brochure, the George Washington Masonic National Memorial's "form was inspired by the lighthouse of Alexandria, Egypt, one of the ancient Seven Wonders of the World" and it "is capped with a pyramid and surmounted by a stylized finial, symbolizing Light." "The Memorial is a beacon that spreads the Light of Freemasonry and the legacy of Washington to the world." It enlightens the world.

From the perspective of someone standing at the GW MM, when the sun rises on the summer solstice, it does so over Cedar Point, RI; when the sun reaches mid-day, 120 degrees south of sunrise, it does so over Cedar Point, NC; and when the sun sets, 120 degrees west of mid-day, it does so over Cedar Point, OH. The sun then rises again 120 degrees to the east. These 120-degree angles indicate that the Cedar Points symbolize an equilateral triangle. The connection of each of these points to the life cycle of the sun (birth, maturity, death, resurrection) indicates that this equilateral triangle symbolizes the Divine Trinity and immortality. Pike: "The equilateral triangle was one of their [the ancient mystic's] symbols; and so was the mystical Y [the chalice]; both alluding to the Triune God, and the latter being the ineffable name [Yahweh] of the Deity." The Solar Trinity in our map looks like a Y, or a chalice (Figure 11). The letter Y is the English representation of the Hebrew letter Yod, which is the first letter in the Hebrew name of the Deity (YHWH). In English-speaking cultures, the Masonic Compass and Square symbol has a G at its center, where G stands for God (or Geometry, which means the Architect, which is God). The true Masonic Compass and Square diagram has not a G at its center, but a Hebrew Yod, which might confuse or offend English speakers. The Y now revealed upon the American landscape represents Freemasonry and its God, the light-radiating all-seeing eye. An appendix to this book diagrams a possible Compass and Square shape on our map. I relegate it to an appendix because my evidence is sketchy (the shape is incomplete) and because the Compass and Square merely supports attribution, which we have already established, and is irrelevant to deciphering our map. Gist: Oak Island conspicuously bears exactly 45 degrees from Cedar Point, NC.

In the Real World...

It is important that we consider whether or not this series of alignments among structures, streets, and symbols is merely a coincidence. I anticipate the following argument being made against my claim that these alignments are proof, beyond all reasonable doubt, of a treasure map concealed in plain sight. One might note that *statistically-speaking* it is *possible* that these alignments are a coincidence. I must acknowledge that this point is true. It is true in the same sense that I cannot *prove* that unicorns do not exist because I have not searched behind every rock on Mars, which is where a unicorn might be hiding right now. Here is my counterargument, which I will call "In the Real World." Let us pretend that we painstakingly, and somewhat humorously, accumulated one million monkeys and gave each one a typewriter with all the blank sheets of paper that any monkey could ever desire. A statistician, thinking only from a sterile mathematical perspective, could calculate what they consider to be the probability that one of these monkeys will type, whilst banging on the typewriter's keys in a seemingly random way, a perfect copy of Shakespeare's First Folio of plays, a notoriously lengthy volume. If one of our monkeys managed to produce a series of lines whose first letters (down the left margin) read "F Bacon," then we should not be too excited, as these are only six lines among thousands. If that name appeared on line 33, which was Francis Bacon's cipher number, then the odds of a miracle had risen dramatically. And if one of our monkeys did indeed produce such a perfect copy, then we might be inclined to marvel at our fortune, having just witnessed an event of high improbability. But, *In the Real World*, we should not be so enthusiastic. Rather, we should immediately launch an investigation to determine how a human being interfered with our experiment and gave one of the monkeys a perfect copy of Shakespeare's First Folio. *In the Real World*, a monkey will never create a perfect copy of Shakespeare's First Folio, no matter how many monkeys are used and no matter how much time they are given. *In the Real World*, it is simply absurd to suggest that our Cedar Point alignments, Tree of Life alignments, solstice alignments, 66-degree occurrences, and the angular and length matches (precise matches) are merely a coincidence. *In the Real World*, human beings did this and we should focus our energy on determining why.

The first appendix is a timeline of events related to the construction and discovery of this map. Here are a few highlights. The boundary of the triangle was started in 1713 with the establishment of Cedar Point, NC. It was completed in 1816 with the Sandusky Plat. Its center was begun by 1749 with the placement of King Street in Alexandria. The center was completed in 1922 with the building of the George Washington Masonic Memorial at the bend in King Street. A due-north line from Cedar Point, NC intersects King Street at this bend. The starting point of the map, Oak Island, predates 1795, likely by decades. The key to the map, the 26-degree center column path in New York City, was started in late 1831, formed in 1857, finished in 1881, and adorned by additional obelisks (skyscrapers) in the 1920s and 30s.

While I consider the existence of the map, as observed from its technical details, to be beyond dispute, its purpose, as revealed through a single Masonic narrative hidden within, will solidify my case.

Part II
Deciphering the Map

Knowledge of Good and Evil

Gold and silver are the gods you adore!
In what are you different from the idolator,
save that he worships one, and you a score?[60]
    - *The Inferno*, Canto XIX

It is clear to me, and I hope to the reader, that a map has been concealed in plain sight on the eastern North American landscape. To be unequivocal on this point, I'll state my position directly: Scottish Rite Freemasons, including George Washington himself, devised and implemented a secret plan to imprint on the New World an encoded symbolism aimed at conveying a specific message. That message goes well beyond mere attribution, e.g., "The Freemasons were here." I call this encoded symbolism a map because it is meaningless without a specific geographic context. It was designed using the Mercator projection, and then enacted with much patience and effort by obtaining property in key places, erecting monuments and buildings as needed, and naming them accordingly. I do not consider this effort (nor my analysis of it) to be complete, but it is far enough along to allow for a meaningful attempt at deciphering the map.

---

[60] Alighieri, Dante. (1954) *The Divine Comedy* (J. Ciardi trans.). NAL, p 153.

There is much speculation about the morality of Freemasonry, including suspicions that at its core it is an evil conspiracy devoted to things like world domination, moral corruption, extraterrestrial concealment, religious subversion, Satan worship—you name it. I am convinced that we have assembled a concealed map, and the fact that it was hidden in plain sight tells me that it was meant to be found. It will lead us to something that Scottish Rite Freemasons intended for someone—*outside* their *inner* circle—to find. Otherwise this secret would only have been passed down by word of mouth, apron-wearing Brother to apron-wearing Brother. In some ways, this map is a time-released message. Its creators could not have expected it to remain unnoticed forever. But its complexity (and incremental implementation) ensured that it would remain hidden for decades, at least. To start, what is the basic attribute of this treasure; is it good, evil, neither, or both?

A cursory examination of nearly any religious system on Earth will lead you to a few basic rules of morality. In the Abrahamic religions of Judaism and Christianity these are the thou-shalt-nots of the Ten Commandments. So as not to incite an atheist protest by listing the Commandments here, I created my own list of precepts.

Thou shalt not:
- Seek advantage through deception,
- Initiate acts of violence or destruction,
- Trespass on another's relationships and property,
- Acquire relationships and property through surreptitious means,
- Influence others into violating these precepts.

Scholars will likely debate the finer points of this list (for generations to come), but it serves to frame my point. I changed, for example, thou shalt not lie to thou shalt not seek advantage through deception. I have found that some folks think that they remain on the good side when they do not actually speak a lie, even if they knowingly lead someone into believing an untruth, which to me is still a lie. I also added a precept, the last one. If I were to approach a child, impressionable and naive as they are, and I convinced that child to steal something for me, would it be the child or me that committed the sin? I did, of course, the adult. The child did not know better. As advertisers, politicians, and cable news networks prove daily, the human mind is ripe for manipulation. I left out the commandments pertaining to false idols and such and will visit them later.

For comparison, what is the Masonic value system? Pike outlined Freemasonry's values in rather plain language in *Morals and Dogma*. According to him, the "practical morality of Freemasonry" is summarized as follows [formatting altered]:

To be true, under whatever temptation to be false;

to be honest in all your dealings, even if great losses should be the consequence;

to be charitable, when selfishness would prompt you to close your hand, and deprivation of luxury or comfort must follow the charitable act;

to judge justly and impartially, even in your own case, when baser impulses prompt you to do an injustice in order that you may be benefited or justified;

to be tolerant, when passion prompts to intolerance and persecution;

to do that which is right, when the wrong seems to promise larger profit; and

to wrong no man of anything that is his, however easy it may seem so to enrich yourself.

Through Freemasonry, Pike claims, "your spiritual nature is taught and encouraged to assert its rightful dominion over your appetites and passions," and you are taught "to overcome the fear of death, to devote yourself to the great cause of civil and religious Liberty, to be the Soldier of all that is just, right, and true." How is it a virtue "to overcome the fear of death?" Pike challenges aspects of the religious constructs:

It is not possible to create a true and genuine Brotherhood upon any theory of the baseness of human nature: nor by a community of belief in abstract propositions as to the nature of the Deity, the number of His persons, or other theorems of religious faith: nor by the establishment of a system of association simply for mutual relief, and by which, in consideration of certain payments regularly made, each becomes entitled to a certain stipend in case of sickness, to attention then, and to the ceremonies of burial after death.

He suggests that Freemasonry differs from these other systems in that it is a true Brotherhood:

> There can be no genuine Brotherhood without mutual regard, good opinion and esteem, mutual charity, and mutual allowance for faults and failings. It is those only who learn habitually to think better of each other, to look habitually for the good that is in each other, and expect, allow for, and overlook, the evil, who can be Brethren one of the other, in any truse [sic] sense of the word. Those who gloat over the failings of one another, who think each other to be naturally base and low, of a nature in which the Evil predominates and excellence is not to be looked for, cannot be even friends, and much less Brethren.

But to enter into consideration for that Brotherhood, one must approach it with a humble mind. Freemasonry requires that Initiates declare a belief in a higher power. I conclude that this declaration is not a religious one, but ensures that the candidate is sufficiently in awe of the vastness of the Universe and is aware of our unending ignorance amid that vastness. Wilmshurst [emphasis added]:

> One qualification above all was essential to the aspirant, as it is still today—humility. The wisdom into which the Mysteries and initiation admit a man is foolishness to the world; it is a reversal and revolution of all orthodox and academic standards. To attain it a man must be prepared for that complete and voluntary self-denial **which may involve his finding negated everything he has previously held to be true, or which those among whom he ordinarily mingles believe to be true**. He must be content to "become a fool for the kingdom of heaven's sake" and to suffer adversity, ridicule and obloquy for it if needs be. This was one of the prime reasons for secrecy and one—though not the only one—of the origins of the Masonic injunction as to secrecy. The world's wisdom and that to which initiation admits are so antipodal in their nature that any intrusion of the latter will infallibly provoke resentment from the former. Hence it is written **"Cast not your pearls before swine, neither give that which is holy unto dogs—lest they turn and rend you."** Silence and secrecy are, therefore, desirable if only in self-defence, though there are other reasons; but humility is indispensable. In the public processions of the Lesser Mysteries—for

the public were permitted at certain festivals to participate to a small extent in some of the more exoteric knowledge—the sacred emblems and eucharistic vessels used in the rites were carried with great reverence upon the back of an ass. With the same intention, it is said that one of the great Greek philosophers always had an ass by his side in his lecture-room when instructing his students. The explanation is given in the words of one of the old authorities upon initiation as follows: "There is no creature so able to receive divinity as an ass, into whom if ye be not turned, ye shall in no wise be able to carry the divine mysteries." In the light of this, one will at once discern the symbolical significance of the Christian Master riding into Jerusalem upon an ass.

Pike's description of Masonic values, as described above, is consistent with other Masonic texts spanning a large breadth of time. It is also consistent with the behavior of America's most famous Freemasons. Did George Washington aspire to virtues such as these? I will continue to pursue the treasure with confidence that its protectors likely possess noble intentions.

Expelled From Paradise

And he [Virgil, Dante's symbol of Reason] replied, seeing my soul in
tears: "He must go by another way who would escape this wilderness,
for that mad beast that fleers before you there, suffers no man to pass....
He will not feed on lands nor loot, but honor and love and wisdom will
make straight his way. He will rise... and in him shall be the resurrection
and new day."[61]

   - *The Inferno*, Canto I

To decipher our map of good intentions we must dive deeper into
Masonic philosophy and symbolism. We need not attempt to decipher all of
Freemasonry, nor judge its meaning, or the meaning of other philosophical
and religious systems. As tempted as the reader might become in this chapter
to inject the reader's own beliefs, such a debate distracts from our purpose
here. Our task is to understand how Freemasonry interprets the symbols in
our map and to use that information to decode the map. The personal beliefs

---

[61] Alighieri, Dante. (1954) *The Divine Comedy* (J. Ciardi trans.). NAL, p 19.

of the author and of the reader are neither required nor desired. Why do I say this? Because everything pertaining to Freemasonry seems to involve the controversial and the crazy. As such, it is only fitting that the first step in our intellectual journey to decipher the map conjures a name that you likely associate with the Devil.

The map begins on Oak Island, where treasure seekers are enticed to descend a pit of nine levels, each formed from oak logs. As I said at the start, I equate these nine levels with Dante's nine circles of hell, as depicted in his *Divine Comedy* consisting of three (a trinity of) parts: *Inferno, Purgatorio, Paradiso*. "Allegorically, the Divine Comedy represents the journey of the soul towards God, with the Inferno describing the recognition and rejection of sin."[62] The *Divine Comedy* is divided into the following number of sub-parts (called Cantos): *Inferno* (33), *Purgatorio* (33), *Paradiso* (33). Manly Hall makes the following observation connecting Dante to the *Sacred Mysteries* (the philosophic predecessor to Freemasonry). Note the similarity of the description of the circle (rose) divided by a cross to our Tree of Life template (Figure 2) [emphasis added].

> Many suspect the Rosicrucian rose to be a conventionalization of the Egyptian and Hindu lotus blossom, with the same symbolic meaning as this more ancient symbol. The Divine Comedy stamps Dante Alighieri as being familiar with the theory of Rosicrucianism. Concerning this point, Albert Pike in his Morals and Dogma makes this significant statement: **"His [Dante's] Hell is but a negative Purgatory.** His heaven is composed of a series of Kabalistic circles, divided by a cross, like the Pantacle of Ezekiel. In the center of this cross blooms a rose, and we see the symbol of the Adepts of the Rose-Croix for the first time publicly expounded and almost categorically explained."

This paragraph links Dante, the Mysteries, and Masonic teaching, at least in Hall's and Pike's minds. Hall revisits Dante, drawing out the point that is relevant to deciphering our map [emphasis added].

> The gloom and depression of the Lesser Mysteries represented the agony of **the spiritual soul unable to express itself because it has accepted the limitations and illusions of the human environment**. The crux of the Eleusinian argument was that man is neither better nor wiser after death than during life. If he does not rise above ignorance during his

---

[62] http://en.wikipedia.org/wiki/Inferno_(Dante)

sojourn here, man goes at death into eternity to wander about forever, making the same mistakes which he made here. **If he does not outgrow the desire for material possessions here, he will carry it with him into the invisible world, where, because he can never gratify the desire, he will continue in endless agony.** Dante's Inferno is symbolically descriptive of the sufferings of those who never freed their spiritual natures from the cravings, habits, viewpoints, and limitations of their Plutonic personalities. **Those who made no endeavor to improve themselves** (whose souls have slept) during their physical lives, passed at death into Hades, where, lying in rows, they slept through all eternity as they had slept through life.

From this perspective, not all of the Beatitudes are complimentary. The meek [of spirit] define their self-worth in material terms. As such, they shall inherit the [material] earth. Those who seek [self-] righteousness shall fulfill themselves [of their own egos].

When I first thumbed through Pike's enormous, dense, and deliberately obscure *Morals and Dogma* I encountered an odd paragraph. Surely, he does not mean what he seems to be saying here [emphasis in original]:

The Apocalypse is, to those who receive the nineteenth Degree, the Apotheosis of that Sublime Faith which aspires to God alone, and despises all the pomps and works of Lucifer. LUCIFER, the *Light-bearer*! Strange and mysterious name to give to the Spirit of Darkness! Lucifer, the Son of the Morning! Is it *he* who bears the *Light*, and with its splendors intolerable blinds feeble, sensual, or selfish Souls? Doubt it not! for traditions are full of Divine Revelations and Inspirations: and Inspiration is not of one Age nor of one Creed.

Look up this passage on the Internet and you will find a tremendous amount of commentary. The most absurd of it uses this passage to "prove" that Freemasons worship Satan. Here is one of my favorites.

After extensive research and reviewing the testimonies of respectable citizens of great credibility, I have come to the conclusion that Freemasonry poses the greatest threat to our society. I have come to the conclusion that Freemasonry is an anti-Christian organization that is involved in organized crime and possibly terrorism throughout the world, and involves its members in anti-Christian occult rituals that defy the Holy Bible. I have also found strong evidence that Freemasonry puts its members into the government and well placed positions to carry out an agenda upon a nation.

Egad! I'll finish writing this book in my zombie-proof bomb shelter, if I'm not already dead. That quote doesn't mention Satan worship specifically, but it was too good to pass up. For those persons that think that Freemasons (even if only the "core" group at the top) worship Satan, I offer two common sense counterarguments. The first is this: do you think that George "I cannot tell a lie" Washington, Teddy "the original progressive" Roosevelt, Franklin "The New Deal" Roosevelt, Harry "the buck stops here" Truman, and Benjamin "Freedom of the Press" Franklin were Satan worshippers, or within miles of them? Do you think that an organization that recruits *millions* of persons based on a message of morality and charity could be run (without discovery) by Satan worshippers? Obviously not. Second, it is simply ridiculous to take six lines of text out of an 850-page book and suggest that those six lines (taken literally) are its core message. Nothing, and I say NOTHING, in Masonic teaching leads me to conclude that these people have anything to do with Devil [Evil] worship. So, what in the world is Pike's Lucifer comment actually about? Freemasonry keeps secrets for a reason. Because I know how this book ends, I can tell you that we are knee deep in one of Freemasonry's biggest secrets.

Please recall my earlier foot-stomping note that if you take anything in Freemasonry literally then you are missing the point. It harbors its secrets within layers of symbols. The reader's definition (or my own) of Lucifer is irrelevant. The fact that you might think that Lucifer is a real entity doing real deeds on Earth is irrelevant to understanding Freemasonry. The pertinent question is this: what does Lucifer *symbolize in Freemasonry?* But first, why again do I think that Lucifer is our next clue?

The most prominent number in the Tree of Life template is 147, with four of its segments having that length. It is also the orientation of the Liberty Island Tree of Life, which points at 147-degrees relative to north and sits atop 14.7 acres of land. You are likely familiar with the association of Satan to the number 666 (the mark of the beast).[63] Lucifer has his own number. Hall [emphasis added]:

Lucifer is the greatest mystery of symbolism. The secret knowledge of the Rosicrucians concerning Lucifer is nowhere so plainly set forth as

---

[63] 666 is the sum of all integers from 1 to 36. 741 is the sum of 1 to 38.

in [some cryptic diagrams], which virtually reveal **his true identity**, a carefully guarded secret about which little has been written. **Lucifer is represented by the number 741**.

I have encoded within the entirety of this text Lucifer's true identity, per the *Mysteries*. In the symbolism and philosophy of the *Mysteries*, there is a difference between Satan (the Deceiver) and Lucifer (the Light Bearer, the Star of Morning). Earlier in this chapter I noted Pike's claim that Hell is a *negative* Purgatory. So, let's reverse the descending number for Lucifer (741) to get the ascending number 147.[64] This is not a coincidence. The first clue to the deliberateness of the reversal is found in the dimensions of the Venus length of our Tree of Life template. Recall from earlier that the center column of the Tree of Life is 1152 feet long, which is 8x144 feet. The width is 5x144 feet, giving the TOL shape an 8-by-5 size. Hall equates the number 144 with "the symbol of salvation." Note its prolific use in the book of *Revelation*. The length of the TOL, being a product of 8, represents Venus, which orbits the Sun 8 times for every 5 times that the Earth orbits the Sun. As such, the width, being a factor of 5, represents the material (Earth) and our five senses. Lucifer is Venus, the "morning star" or "son of the morning." From *Isaiah* 14-12:

> How art thou fallen from heaven, O Lucifer, son of the morning! *how* art thou cut down to the ground, which didst weaken the nations![65]

Which of the planets' astrological signs is a circle (rose) and a cross (the rose cross)? Venus (♀). Venus, the brightest object in the sky (except for the Sun and Moon), does an interesting dance with the Sun. Wikipedia:

> Venus "overtakes" Earth every 584 days as it orbits the Sun. As it does so, it changes from the "Evening Star," visible after sunset, to the "Morning Star," visible before sunrise.... Venus was known to ancient civilizations both as the "morning star" and as the "evening star," names that reflect the early assumption that these were two separate objects. The Venus tablet of Ammisaduqa, dated 1581 BCE, shows the Babylonians understood the two were a single object, referred to in the tablet as the **"bright queen of the sky,"** and could support this view with detailed observations. The Greeks thought of the two as separate stars, Phosphorus and Hesperus, until the time of Pythagoras in the sixth

---

[64] The descending numbers 7-4-1 are each separated by 3, which embeds 33 in 741. Similarly, 33 is embedded in the ascending numbers 1-4-7.

[65] Isaiah 14-12, *The Bible*. King James Version.

century BC. The Romans designated the morning aspect of Venus as Lucifer, literally "Light-Bringer," and the evening aspect as Vesper, both literal translations of the respective Greek names.[66] [emphasis added] Therefore, through its association with Venus, the center column of the TOL template is associated with Lucifer (and not Satan, which is different). So, the center column represents Venus, and Venus is Lucifer. What again is the center column? Here is Hall's quote from earlier:

> Three vertical columns support the universal system as typified by the Sephirothic Tree [of Life]. The central pillar has its foundation in Kether [point 1], the Eternal One. It passes downward through the hypothetical Sephira, Daath [Knowledge point], and then through Tiphereth [point 6] and Jesod [point 9], with its lower end resting upon the firm foundation of Malchuth [point 10], the last of the globes. The true import of the central pillar is equilibrium. It demonstrates how the Deity always manifests by emanating poles of expression from the midst of Itself but remaining free from the illusion of polarity [Meaning: the Deity is neither Good nor Evil, but both *and* neither]. If the numbers of the four Sephiroth connected by this column be added together (1 +6 +9 + 10), the sum is 26, the number of Jehovah.

Does the transitive property suggest, then, that Freemasonry considers Lucifer to be Jehovah (God)? No. As we'll soon see, Lucifer is present *on* the center column, but is not the entire center column.

The second clue to the connection of our TOL to Lucifer (the Light Bearer) is the segments that form the center column. Recall that in my rendering of the Tree of Life it contains a Compass and Square that are split by the center column. Pike tells us to stay on this center path: "[W]henever you depart from the centre of the Square and the Compass you will no longer be able to work with success." It is 1152 feet long and is composed of six segments, four that are 147 feet in length and two that are 282 feet in length. 147 = 3x49, where 49 is the square of the "sacred" number seven.[67] 282 = 3x94. 94 is 49 reversed, just as 147 is 741 reversed ("Hell is but a negative Purgatory"). This is not a coincidence, especially given the Venus-Lucifer connection, and the existence of Dante's nine levels of Hell beneath the Oak Island Tree of Life. Note that each of these numbers is a Trinity (three times 49 and 94). Our TOL template is telling us that our path begins with Lucifer.

---

[66] http://en.wikipedia.org/wiki/Venus

[67] A 7x7 magic square is associated with Venus, per Agrippa's *Occult Philosophy*.

Unfortunately, this is a complicated and obscure topic of enormous controversy. But, since I'm writing this chapter last and I know how this ends, I can cut through to the points relevant to deciphering our map. Sip your hot tea in comfort, pinky finger confidently extended, trusting that we will not end up within miles of anything resembling Devil [Evil] worship (or any other kind of worship, for that matter).

We now know that Lucifer is Venus, but a more specific identity (present on our map) will be revealed later. Hint: Pike italicized the word he in his Lucifer quote above for a reason. For now, we need to consider *what* is Lucifer (symbolically).

But first, I need to be certain that you agree that the symbol of Lucifer is the key to deciphering our map. Turn back a few pages and take another look at Figure 17, which I called "Inverted Triangle of the 33rd Degree with Paths of the Sun." It is an inverted triangle with two diagonal lines crossing over its center. Now compare Figure 17 (and Figure 18) with the figure at the top of this chapter. They are the same symbol. The V at the bottom purportedly stands for Verum (Latin for truth). I suspect that it also stands for Venus. The symbol at the top of this chapter, which is what our inverted triangle map clearly represents, is the *Seal of Lucifer* imprinted on the Land of the Free.[68] The reason behind this bizarre act reveals the purpose of our quest. Wilmshurst gives the next clue [emphasis added]:

> [T]he [Masonic] candidate learns from his superior brethren, that they, along with himself, are in search of something that is lost and which they have hopes of finding. And it is here that the great motive of this and of all quests, as well as the clue to the real purpose of Masonry, appears prominently and is stated in emphatic terms. **Masonry is the quest after something that has been lost.** Now what is it that has been lost? Consider the matter thus. Why should we, or the world at large, require systems of religion and philosophy at all? What is the motive and reason for the existence of a Masonic Order and of many other Orders of Initiation, both of the past and the present? Why should they exist at all? ...every man in his reflective moments realizes the sense of some element of his own being having become lost; that he is conscious, if he be honest with himself, of the sense of moral imperfection, of ignorance, of restricted knowledge about himself and his surroundings; that he is

---

[68] http://en.wikipedia.org/wiki/Lucifer. Also see the *Gremorium Verum*.

aware, in short, of some radical deficiency in his constitution, which, were it but found and made good, would satisfy this craving for information, for completeness and perfection, would "**lead him from darkness to light**," and would put him beyond ignorance and beyond the touch of the many ills that flesh is heir to. The point is too obvious to need pressing further, and the answer to it is... popularly known as the Fall of Man.... [I]n this present world of ours [humanity] is undergoing a period of restriction, of ignorance, of discipline and experience, that shall ultimately fit him to return to the centre whence he came and to which he properly belongs.

"Lead him from darkness to light." We now know *who* brings the light: the light-bearer. Let's uncover *what* brings the light.

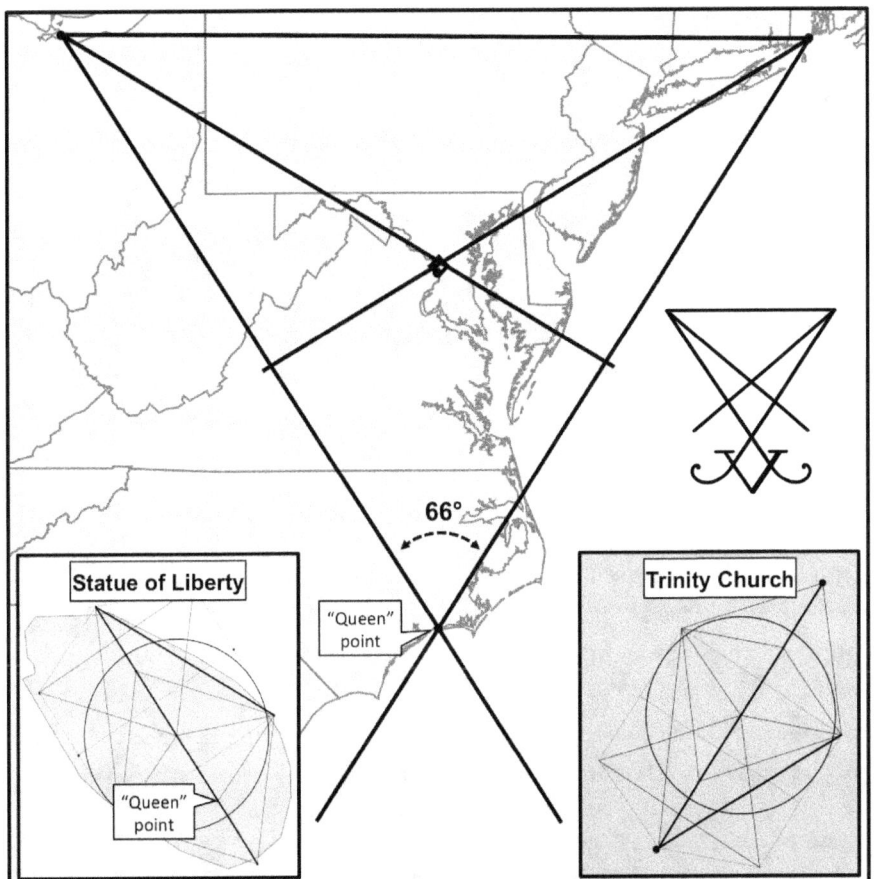

Figure 18: Figure 17 redrawn with "Queen" point [9] at Cedar Point, NC

"Liberty Enlightening the World"

O Sovereign Wisdom, how Thine art doth shine
in Heaven, on Earth, and in the Evil World!
How justly doth Thy power judge and assign![69]
    -*The Inferno*, Canto XIX

They are forever free who renounce all selfish desires and break away
from the ego-cage of "I," "me," and "mine" to be united with the Lord.
This is the supreme state. Attain to this and pass from death to
immortality.[70]
    -*The Bhagavad Gita*

At this point, I need to make it abundantly clear to the reader that I am
not a Freemason, nor do I know any that I am aware of. I am not held
captive by their vows. I do not present here a pro-Masonic or anti-Masonic
message. I am striving to distill for the reader a vast cacophony of ideas and
conspiracies about Freemasonry so that we may accurately decipher the map
that is clearly placed upon our landscape by Scottish Rite Freemasons,

---

[69] Alighieri, Dante. (1954) *The Divine Comedy* (J. Ciardi trans.). NAL, p 150.
[70] *The Bhagavad Gita* (E. Easwaran trans.). (1985). Nigiri Press, p. 69.

including Masons of tremendous reputation and importance, such as George Washington. If George is talking, then my mouth is shut and I am listening. When he is finished, only then will I independently consider his ideas—in total—and decide for myself where I stand.

Freemasonry at its core offers an alternative interpretation of religious narratives. I do not see in Freemasonry an attempt to *challenge* religion, but only to offer an alternative perspective to those seeking it actively. Its ideas are likely to prompt a defensive response by some religious adherents. I caution against such an inclination. If one is confident in one's beliefs then one need not worry about scrutiny. Einstein did not attack those that questioned his theories. Yet his ideas persisted, despite harsh scrutiny, because they were backed by reputable facts and solid logic. Alternatively, modern Islamic extremists are a stark example of a broken ideology, one that requires violence, intimidation, and bribery to keep it alive. Freemasons do not recruit and their philosophies are not universal facts. They use symbols defined in a manner to convey their philosophy about humankind's role in the universe, and the purpose of human life. Wilmshurst: "[T]he literally-minded never see behind the letter of the allegory. The truly initiated mind discerns the allegory's spiritual value." It seems obvious to me that if Christians and non-Christians alike were to practice the teachings and example of Jesus that the world would be a better place. I think that the same can be said about most religious doctrines that promote morality, community, and humility. The same can be said of Freemasonry. If their philosophy and rituals bring more people into a life of morality, community, and humility, then we are all better for it. As irritating as differences of opinion may be at times, they are not a threat to a well-formed idea. No idea born of an infinite wisdom requires a human to interpret or defend it.

Freemason philosophy seems clearly Lucifer-centric, wherein Lucifer is defined not as an agent of evil, but as the human spirit of reason—that God-given part of us that debates the ideas of others. As such, Lucifer is the agent of Liberty. Pike [emphasis in original]:

> The true name of Satan, the Kabalists say, is that of Yahveh reversed; for Satan is not a black god, but the negation of God. The Devil [to the Kabalists] is the personification of Atheism or Idolatry. For the [Masonic] Initiates, this is not a *Person*, but a *Force*, created for good, but which *may* serve for evil. *It is the instrument of Liberty or Free Will.* They represent this Force, which presides over the physical generation

[material world], under the mythologic and horned form of the God PAN; thence came the he-goat of the Sabbat, brother of the Ancient Serpent, and the Light-bearer or *Phosphor*, of which the poets have made the false Lucifer of the legend.

"Created for good, but which may serve for evil." Pike is not worshipping evil, as some claim, but is arguing that its existence is inseparable from the existence of good, and he is acknowledging liberty (free will) as its source, and the material world its domain.

One cannot be a Free Man if one is beholden, without scrutiny, to the ideas of another. The false idol of the Ten Commandments need not be a statue of the sun god; it could be a charming politician seeking a vote, a sports icon seeking a sly favor, or a friend that takes advantage of a fragile ego. Shakespeare: "Let not my love be called idolatry." Wikipedia: "Luciferianism is a belief system that venerates the essential characteristics that are affixed to Lucifer. The tradition, influenced by Gnosticism, usually reveres Lucifer not as the Devil, but as a liberator or guiding spirit." (Freemasons are not "Luciferians." To them Lucifer is a symbol, not a supernatural being.) This independent force within all persons is the genesis of liberty, but only if it is used. I ask the reader: What do you *believe* and why do you believe it? How much have you scrutinized your beliefs? Are they *your* beliefs or those of someone else? A core secret of Freemasonry is that it equates such scrutiny, of all things and not only religion, with liberty—individual sovereignty. Pike: "It is not enough for a people to *gain* its liberty. It must *secure* it. It must not intrust it to the keeping, or hold it at the pleasure, of any one man [idol]." God is the origin, not only of good, but also of evil; it is in this choice that liberty is defined. Without the capacity for evil there is no choice, and without choice there is no liberty. Pike [emphasis added; capitalization in original]:

> God gives to man the Soul or Intelligence, which exists before the body, and which he unites with the body. The reasoning Principle comes from God through the Word, and communes with God and with the Word; but there is also in man an irrational Principle, that of the inclinations and passions which produce disorder, **emanating from inferior spirits who fill the air as ministers of God**. The body, taken from the Earth, and the irrational Principle that animates it concurrently with the rational Principle, are hated by God, while the rational soul which He has given it, is, as it were, **captive in this prison**, this coffin, that encompasses it.

The present condition of man is not his primitive condition, when he was the image of the Logos [infinite Deity]. He has fallen from his first estate [perfect creation]. But he may raise himself again, by following the directions of WISDOM and of the Angels [rational faculties] which God has commissioned to aid him in freeing himself from the bonds of the body, and combating **Evil, the existence whereof God has permitted, to furnish him [Man] the means of exercising his liberty**. The souls that are purified, not by the Law [adherence to commandments] but by light [reasoned Truth], rise to the Heavenly regions, to enjoy there a perfect felicity [I'll explain Heaven in a bit].

Liberty (sovereignty) is the first emanation of the Deity and the beginning of our quest, represented to Freemasons through the first Sephiroth (point [1]) of the Qabalah Tree of Life. Pike [emphasis added]:

As such, it [the infinite Deity] has revealed itself in ten emanations or Sephiroth [of the Tree of Life], which are not ten different beings, nor even beings at all; but sources of life, vessels of Omnipotence, and types of Creation. They are **Sovereignty or Will** [1], Wisdom [2], Intelligence [3], Benignity [4], Severity [5], Beauty [6], Victory [7], Glory [8], Permanency [9], and Empire [10]. **These are attributes of God; and this idea, that God reveals Himself by His attributes, and that the human mind cannot perceive or discern God Himself**, in his works, but only his mode of manifesting Himself, is a profound Truth.

As the agent of liberty (sovereignty), Lucifer is the first Sephiroth, the anchor of the center column of the Tree of Life. In Freemasonry, liberty comes from reason, which Freemasonry calls the spirit or the soul. So, "spiritual development" is code for intellectual development. Belief is insufficient; one must contemplate the what and the why. The essence of the Infinite Deity is not that of a human form, a father figure possessed of human emotions like anger and jealousy, but is that of Reason: ordered, balanced, and unjudging. This idea is why Freemasonry calls itself a science. Pike [bold added; capitalization in original]:

To believe in the Reason of God, and in the God of Reason, is to make Atheism impossible. **It is the Idolaters who have made the Atheists.** Analogy gives the Sage all the forces of Nature. It is the key of the Grand Arcanum, the root of the Tree of Life, the science of Good and Evil.

> **The Absolute [Deity], is REASON**. Reason IS, by means of Itself. It IS BECAUSE IT IS, and not because we suppose it. IT IS, where nothing exists; but nothing could possibly exist without IT. **Reason is Necessity, Law, the Rule of all Liberty**, and the direction of every Initiative. If God IS, HE IS by Reason. **The conception of an Absolute Deity, outside of, or independent of, Reason, is the IDOL of Black Magic**, the PHANTOM of the Demon.
>
> The Supreme Intelligence is necessarily rational. God, in philosophy, can be no more than a Hypothesis; but a Hypothesis imposed by good sense on Human Reason. **To personify the Absolute Reason, is to determine the Divine Ideal**.

Liberty reveals truth, which Freemasonry calls light. Truth is found within one's rational faculties ("reasoning Principle") and not within one's passions ("irrational Principle"), or in the beliefs of others. Following others leads to tyranny, as it is within all persons to abuse the power that they gain over others. Those who abuse their influence practice evil. Therefore, those who follow them, and give them strength through numbers, inadvertently, or neglectfully, give strength to evil. Independence from the control of others is not a right—*it is an obligation*! Independence—through reasoned analysis—is the only means to lessen the collective power of evil, of which the world will never be rid. The Good encourage humble community-focused independence and the Evil encourage followership and subjugation to empower their own agenda, beliefs, and wants. It is not a coincidence that there are five times the amount of psychopaths in positions of high leadership (politicians, business executives) as there are among the normal population.[71] Evil controls. Good inspires.

This concept of Liberty reveals it to be interdependent. In a community with even one slave there are no masters, only slaves in different skins. Consider the manipulative media personality who must expend so much effort stoking the flames of their impassioned audience, or the politician swaying in the winds of public opinion that are fanned by divisive and fearful rhetoric. These persons bask in their power over the collective, but they are also enslaved by its fickle whims. "The divine qualities lead to freedom; the demonic, to bondage."[72] Pike learned this lesson through experience. As I

---

[71] Ronson, Jon. (2011) *The Psychopath Test: A Journey Through the Madness Industry*. Penguin Publishing Group. Kindle Edition, p. 162.

[72] *The Bhagavad Gita* (E. Easwaran trans.). (1985). Nigiri Press, p. 190.

mentioned in an earlier chapter, Pike acknowledged the evil of slavery, yet served the army that defended it. He lived in a society whose culture and economy depended on the persistence of evil, and he likely feared to challenge it. Would you stand alone against an injustice committed against others, no matter the cost? The fear of death can be a powerful motivator. A society that becomes rigid in its heritage and in its structure is unable to challenge manifestations of that culture, no matter how despicable they may be. The people are enslaved by the collective status quo.

The idea of America, Land of the Free, brought this concept of liberty, in an obligatory sense, into the open human consciousness. Pike [emphasis in original]:

> Truths are the springs from which duties flow; and it is but a few
> hundred years since a new Truth began to be distinctly seen; that MAN
> IS SUPREME OVER INSTITUTIONS, AND NOT THEY OVER
> HIM. Man has *natural* empire over *all* institutions. They are for him,
> according to his development; not he for them. This seems to us a very
> simple statement, one to which all men, everywhere, ought to assent.
> But once it was a great new Truth,—not revealed until governments had
> been in existence for at least five thousand years. Once revealed, it
> imposed new duties on men. Man owed it to *himself* to be free. He owed
> it to his country to seek to give *her* freedom, or maintain her in that
> possession. It made Tyranny and Usurpation the enemies of the Human
> Race.

Given that our map began taking shape no later than 1713 with the establishment of Cedar Point, NC, this emphasis within Freemasonry of liberty for the individual and for the people suggests that the American Revolution was a plan set into motion generations before the onset of a violent rebellion, and that the site of its future capital was already decided. This map could only have been implemented after it had been conceived in its entirety, as all points on the map are precisely aligned with several other points. Cedar Point, NC, for example, has 33-degree alignments with the other Cedar Points, a due north alignment with Shuter's Hill, and a 45-degree alignment with Oak Island. Shuter's Hill is aligned with King St, two Cedar Points, and the Newport Tower. The Seal of Lucifer was planned before 1713, and that seal is *Free*masonry's symbol of liberty and self-determination.

In contemporary Christian tradition, Lucifer seems most likely to find association with the Fall of Man, which is the central question of

Freemasonry. So let's examine the place where it occurred: the Garden of Eden. Many, if not most, passages in religious texts, such as the Bible, lend themselves to non-traditional interpretations if viewed symbolically and not literally. The story of the Fall of Man is no exception. What follows is, to me, a plausible Masonic interpretation of the Genesis story, based on the symbols and texts of Freemasonry.

The God of the Garden of Eden was not the infinite creator. He lacked infinite knowledge (not knowing of Adam's and Eve's betrayal), and he lacked infinite control (the serpent perverted his environment). But he was powerful, and he punished those who defied him. In the Garden of Eden he offered his guests material and sensory satisfaction. His guests were offered these comforts and protections in exchange for their soul (in the Masonic sense of the word), their God-given rational spirit. As long as they did not question His rules and eat from the Tree of Knowledge of Good and Evil (choice), then they were welcome. But as soon as they thought for themselves (and exercised free will) they were banished to fend for themselves, to work and survive on the fruits of their own labor. The Garden of Eden was a prison and the prisoners were held willingly through appealing promises and comfort. Hall called it "the illusionary garden of worldly things." Would the reader be willing to trade certain freedoms for a large sum of money or guarantees of comfort and security? When Lucifer was banished from Heaven was it for evil behavior or for insubordination, an act of liberty? The god of the Garden of Eden represents in Freemasonry that aspect of humanity that seeks comfort in the senses and in the material, that which abdicates liberty for a reward: "an irrational Principle, that of the inclinations and passions which produce disorder, emanating from inferior spirits who fill the air as ministers of God."[73] The Garden of Eden is a metaphor for your earthly body, a prison for your spirit, jailed by your passions and desires. That so many proudly seek it is the sustenance of evil in our world. Lucifer represents in Freemasonry that aspect of humanity that seeks liberty from this prison and purpose and immortality through rational action.

In this interpretation of the Garden of Eden, it is a place for the selfish. Recall Pike's Lucifer quote: "Is it *he* who bears the *Light* [truth], and with its splendors intolerable blinds feeble, sensual, or selfish Souls?" The selfish abdicate responsibility (choice, liberty) in exchange for sensual satisfaction. A

---

[73] Pike, Albert. (1871) *Morals and Dogma.*

common view of Heaven is similar. If one lives according to certain rules (set by others) then they will be rewarded with an eternity filled with whatever their heart desires. One is not encouraged to live humbly and for the benefit of humankind, but to follow rules in exchange for a reward. Obviously this is an exaggeration for many, merely an undercurrent, but it is a reality for enough.

Pike equates the terms Soul and Spirit in Masonry to our intellectual capacity and defines it as our core being, that which exists beyond the material world and is imprisoned by our selfish earthly bodies [bold added]:

It is enough for us to know, what Masonry teaches, that we are not all mortal; that the Soul or Spirit, the intellectual and reasoning portion of ourself, is our Very Self, is not subject to decay and dissolution, but is simple and immaterial, survives the death of the body, and is capable of immortality; that it is also *capable* of improvement and advancement, of increase of knowledge of the things that are divine, of **becoming wiser and better, and more and more worthy of immortality**; and that to become so, and to help to improve and benefit others and all our race, is the noblest ambition and highest glory that we can entertain and attain unto, in this momentary and imperfect life.

He continues [emphasis added]:

Every Degree of the Ancient and Accepted Scottish Rite, from the first to the thirty-second, teaches by its ceremonial as well as by its instruction, that **the noblest purpose of life and the highest duty of a man are to strive incessantly and vigorously to win the mastery of everything, of that which in him is spiritual and divine [Reason], over that which is material and sensual**; so that in him also, as in the Universe which God governs, Harmony and Beauty may be the result of a just equilibrium [the center column of the Tree of Life].

Accomplishing this gives us our independence, denying subjugation to our internal temptations and our tendency toward subjugation to others (idols), which adds to the collective power of manipulative (evil) beings. Pike [emphasis added]:

The Science [of Freemasonry] is a real one only for those who admit and understand the philosophy and the religion; and **its process will succeed only for the Adept who has attained the sovereignty of will [the starting point of the Tree of Life], and so become the King of**

the elementary world: for the grand agent of the operation of the Sun [which shines its own light].

Reason liberates; liberty enlightens. Only when each person attains for themself liberty, sovereignty from the control of and the need to control others, does society attain equality. The Seal of Lucifer formed by our Cedar Points is the *Seal of Liberty* stamped upon the Land of the Free, a title that cannot be granted, but must be earned—every day anew. To my abbreviated list of precepts I add one about false idols: Do not abdicate your intellectual and material sovereignty, nor diminish that of another.

Some are unwilling to follow this precept, and they choose to remain vulnerable—an enabler for Evil. For them, the *Sacred Mysteries* use a different approach.

The Ruse

Blessed be He who in His own hand holds all sovereignty: He has power over all things. He created death and life that He might put you to the proof and find out which of you acquitted himself best.[74]

    - *The Koran*

They think the Day of Judgement is far off: but We see it near at hand.... The fire shall drag [the sinner] down by the scalp, shall claim him who had turned his back and amassed riches and covetously hoarded them....

    Not so the worshippers,...

Who set aside a due portion of their wealth for the beggar and for the deprived,... Who restrain their carnal desire....

    These [followers] shall be laden with honours, in fair gardens.... Such is the day with which they are threatened.[75]

    - *The Koran*

---

[74] "Sovereignty," *The Koran* (N.J. Dawood trans). (1995). Penguin Classics.
[75] "The Ladders," *The Koran* (N.J. Dawood trans). (1985). Penguin Classics.

If the people never fear death,

    what is the purpose of threatening to kill them?

If the people ever fear death,

    and I were to capture and kill those who are devious,

    who would dare to be so?

If the people must be ever fearful of death,

    then there will always be an executioner.[76]

    - Tao Te Ching

No man can make another man to be his slave, unless that other hath first enslaved himself

    to life and death,

    to pleasure or pain,

    to hope or fear;

command these passions, and you are freer than the Parthian Kings.

    - Morals and Dogma

[God] is incapable of Anger; higher above any such feelings than the distant stars are above the earth. Bad men do not die because God hates them. They die because it is best for them that they should do so.... Darkness and gloom lie upon the paths of men. They stumble at difficulties, are ensnared by temptations, and perplexed by trouble. They are anxious, and troubled, and fearful. Pain and affliction and sorrow often gather around the steps of their earthly pilgrimage. All this is written indelibly upon the tablets of the human heart.

    It is not to be erased;

    but Masonry sees and reads it in a new light.

It does not expect these ills and trials and sufferings to be removed from life; but that the great truth will at some time be believed by all men,

    that they are the means,

    selected by infinite wisdom,

    to purify the heart, and

    to invigorate the soul whose inheritance is immortality,

and the world its school.

    - Morals and Dogma

---

[76] Lao-Tzu. (1990) *Tao Te Ching* (V.H. Mair trans.). Bantam Books.

Above the bust of Albert Pike at the Scottish Rite House of the Temple is engraved this quote: "What we have done for ourselves alone dies with us. What we have done for others and the world remains and is immortal." A core occupation of Freemasonry pertains to the attainment of immortality. Nearly all Freemasons never grasp its true meaning or the path to it. Wilmshurst [emphasis added]:

> [Freemasonry's] meaning is not discernible all at once, and **unless our minds are properly prepared** and our understandings carefully trained, they [individual Freemasons] are unlikely ever to participate in the real secrets and mysteries of Masonry at all, however often we may watch the performance of external ceremonial or however proficient we may be in memorizing the rituals and instruction lectures. The first stage, the first conception of what Masonry involves, is concerned merely with the **surface-value of the doctrine;** with an acquaintance with the **literal side** of the imparted knowledge which we all obtain upon entering the Craft. **Beyond this stage the vast majority of Masons, it is to be feared, never passes**. This is the stage of knowledge in which the Craft is regarded as a social, semi-public, semi-secret community to which it is agreeable and advantageous to belong for sociable or even for ulterior purposes; in which the goal of the Mason's ambition is to attain office and high preferment and to wear a breastful of decorations; in which he takes a **literal, superficial and historic view** of the subject-matter of the doctrine; in which ability to perform the ceremonial work with dignity and effectiveness and to know the instruction catechisms by heart, so that not a syllable is wrongly rendered, is deemed the height of Masonic proficiency; and where, after discharging these functions with a certain degree of credit, his idea is often to have the Lodge closed as speedily as may be and get away to the relaxation of the festive board.

Openly, Freemasonry employs the ruse as a means of protecting its secrets, such as masking its messages behind a veil of symbols. Behind the veil, it employs the ruse as a means of provoking well-intentioned action. Here is the first such ruse.

The ruse of immortality can be described imperfectly as follows. The (overwhelming) majority of persons consider little during their lifetimes beyond their personal needs and wants. They live selfish lives, viewing society and their environment through a selfish lens. Even their charitable deeds are done from a selfish perspective. They are the politicians who claim service to their communities while amassing personal power and wealth, yet sacrificing little to nothing. Is service not defined by sacrifice? They are the public figure that *performs* acts of charity only in front of a camera. They are the common man who ensures that his donation is visibly paid. Jesus identifies them: "And when you pray, do not be like the hypocrites, for they love to pray on the street corners to be seen by men."[77] But what if we could convince them that there is a Santa Clause, a mythical being that is always watching and judging. And if they follow a series of rules well enough, they will be given access to a wonderful place where they will be showered for eternity with everything they ever wanted—a selfish man's paradise. Then perhaps, just maybe, these selfish souls might follow enough of the rules to do some good during their lifetimes for their fellow man.

Many persons believe that such a literal Paradise exists, and I do not challenge the notion here. Rather, I conclude that the creators of the *Sacred Mysteries*, such as Freemasonry, do not believe in such a place. They promote the ruse for the profane. Wilmshurst: "There has always existed an external, elementary, popular doctrine which has served for the instruction of the masses who are insufficiently prepared for deeper teaching." Freemasonry has a more grounded opinion of immortality. Pike:

> The true Mason labors for the benefit of those who are to come after him, and for the advancement and improvement of his race. That is a poor ambition which contents itself within the limits of a single life. All men who deserve to live, desire to survive their funerals, and to live afterward in the good that they have done mankind, rather than in the fading characters written in men's memories.

The profane pursue eternal life for selfish reasons and through selfish means. Their goal pertains to themselves. Masonry treats this idea of an eternal spirit symbolically, while speaking of it as an actual fact. But at its core it is a ruse. If the profane, the person of closed mind and selfish goals, can be convinced that occasional good deeds will lead them to an eternal afterlife in Paradise then perhaps they will inadvertently achieve an eternal spirit, one that will transcend their lifetime as others benefit from a faint positive mark left on their community.

What is an eternal spirit? Pike: "It is the Dead that govern. The Living only obey." He describes a number of persons throughout history whose

---

[77] Matthew 6:5, *Holy Bible: New International Version*. (1984). International Bible Society.

actions remain felt in modern times. In the Masonic symbolism of building tools, he evokes the imagery of society being built slowly over time by the deeds of the now dead. He says:

> We know not who among the Dead control our destinies. The universal human race is linked and bound together by those influences and sympathies, which in the truest sense do make men's fates. Humanity is the unit, of which the man is but a fraction. What other men in the Past have done, said, thought, makes the great iron network of circumstance that environs and controls us all. We take our faith on trust.

Immortality, as it is defined by Freemasonry, begins to take shape [emphasis added]:

> Thus we obey the dead; and thus shall the living, when we are dead, for weal or woe, obey us. The Thoughts of the Past are the Laws of the Present and the Future. That which we say and do, if its effects last not beyond our lives, is unimportant. **That which shall live when we are dead, as part of the great body of law enacted by the dead**, is the only act worth doing, the only Thought worth speaking. The desire to do something that shall benefit the world, when neither praise nor obloquy will reach us where we sleep soundly in the grave, is the noblest ambition entertained by man.

Wilmshurst: "It [Freemasonry] supplies a need to those who are earnestly enquiring into the purpose and destiny of human life." Freemasonry offers to walk its initiates up three steps, the "three-fold heritage [of Masonry], LIBERTY, EQUALITY, and FRATERNITY."[78] Liberty is the attainment of individual sovereignty over one's own fears and desires. Equality is the result of widespread sovereignty, wherein individuals avoid enslavement by manipulative others. It also stems from the acceptance of our differences and the realization of our personal inferiority when compared to all of society and to the Infinite Deity. Fraternity is the result of Free Men realizing the benefits of sacrificing themselves for the betterment of the human race—a community of Free Men working for one another. Pike [emphasis added]:

> It is the ambition of a true and genuine Mason. **Knowing the slow processes by which the Deity brings about great results**, he does not expect to reap as well as sow, in a single lifetime. It is the inflexible fate and noblest destiny, with rare exceptions, of the great and good, to work,

---

[78] Pike, Albert. (1871) *Morals and Dogma.*

and **let others reap the harvest of their labors**. He who does good, only to be repaid in kind, or in thanks and gratitude, or in reputation and the world's praise, is like him who loans his money, that he may, after certain months, receive it back with interest. To be repaid for eminent services with slander, obloquy, or ridicule, or at best with stupid indifference or cold ingratitude, as it is common, so it is no misfortune, except to those who lack the wit to see or sense to appreciate the service, or the nobility of soul to thank and reward with eulogy, the benefactor of his kind. **His influences live, and the great Future will obey**; whether it recognize or disown the lawgiver.

Pike: "The removal to the Happy Islands [eternal paradise] could only be understood mythically; everything earthly must die." Immortality is the great ruse. It is a noble attempt to bribe the selfish masses into limiting the harm that they will cause to the eternal quest for a human Fraternity by relentlessly pursuing their own desires. The Y on our map, the three-fold lifecycle of the sun, represents this quest for immortality in each of us and in all of US. Every branch of the Y represents a phase of life: birth, maturity, decay, and resurrection. The use of the evergreen—cedar—at the points further supports this conclusion. To Freemasonry, immortality is the echo of one's contribution to the building of a lasting human Fraternity and not a reward for obedience.

Freemasonry derives its philosophy from the sources of the *Sacred Mysteries*. Its link to the Qabalah is overt and well documented in this book. It has another primary source, one less obvious that I have introduced quietly. The Qabalah gives Freemasonry its philosophic structure; *The Bhagavad Gita* (Hindu) gives Freemasonry its soul. The *Gita*, which is a philosophical text of Hinduism, rather than a doctrinal one, begins with a chapter entitled "The War Within," the battle between one's material and spiritual aspects, symbolized in the *Gita* by a civil war. The *Gita* begins its journey to win this war in the next chapter, which is titled "The Illumined Man" and reads in part: "They live in wisdom who see themselves in all and all in them, who have renounced every selfish desire and sense craving tormenting the heart. Neither agitated by grief nor hankering after pleasure, they live free from lust and fear and anger. Established in meditation [reasoned contemplation], they are truly wise."[79] Do you see the connection with Freemasonry? We now

---

[79] *The Bhagavad Gita* (E. Easwaran trans.). (1985). Nigiri Press, p. 68.

understand how Freemasonry defines immortality. How does it interpret rebirth? Through the *Gita*, one observes that the stark difference between Freemasonry and religion is less in their differing perceptions of God than in their differing treatments of death.

Most important among all of the things that the reader should seek to understand is this:

You are going to die.

Realizing this fact is Freemasonry's genesis of liberation, "to overcome the fear of death," to choose the eternity of humankind over the ephemeral self. Said the Buddha: "But if there is no other world and there is no fruit and ripening of actions well done or ill done, then here and now in this life I shall be free from hostility, affliction, and anxiety, and I shall live happily." Accept the inevitability and permanence of your death and you will be free. Pike learned this virtue when he acted to defend slavery, an evil that he had spoken against, because he feared to challenge it, enslaved by the status quo.

Differing from death, the meaning of resurrection (rebirth) is glimpsed within this Buddhist meditation: "Since death alone is certain and the time of death uncertain, what should I do?" Our map reflects this question in the number 66. The *Bhagavad Gita* sets the stage [emphasis added]:

There are two paths which the soul may follow at the time of death. **One leads to rebirth and the other to liberation**. The six months of the northern path of the sun [spring, summer], the path of light, of fire, of day, of the bright fortnight, leads knowers of [Truth] to the supreme goal. The six months of the southern path of the sun [autumn, winter], the path of smoke, of night, of the dark fortnight, leads other souls to the [reflected] light of the moon and to rebirth.

(There are 26 fortnights in a year.) The Equator is the centerline of the Earth; half above and half below. The solstices are the extreme points of the year on which the shortest and longest daylight is seen. For someone standing on the Equator, the sun rises on the summer solstice a fraction of a degree above 66 degrees. The sun rises on the winter solstice a fraction of a degree below 114 degrees. The sun rises on the equinoxes at 90 degrees, due east, the days of balance. As such, this person is never more than 24 degrees from equilibrium, as symbolized by the equinoxes (90-24=66, 90+24=114). So, what does the *Gita* mean by death and rebirth?

Hinduism is perhaps best known in the Western world for its belief in the endless cycles of death and rebirth. These deaths are not at the end of one's material life, as commonly interpreted, but symbolize the death of every moment and the birth of a new choice. Resurrection (rebirth) is a continuous series of choices, each dying to reveal the next. Realizing the impermanence of your life and choosing to help build a permanent human fraternity leads to "liberation," whereas narrow-minded choices lead to rebirth (a cycle of enslavement to frivolous desires and fears). Immortality after a literal death is the sum of this series of rebirths (choices). Your life is defined by the sum of your choices.

Symbolically, the number 66 and our Cedar Points triangle might reflect these choices as follows. On the equinoxes, the days of balance and harmony on which the day sees 12 hours of light and 12 hours of darkness, the sun rises due east, at 90 degrees. This moment represents the balanced path of enlightenment. Because every new day offers an opportunity to begin anew, one is never more than one day (24 hours) from this 90-degree path. In this sense, 66 degrees marks one extreme limit of our imperfection, revealing our continuous opportunity to seek enlightenment (90-24 = 66). In the other direction, the limit of our imperfection is given by 114 degrees (90+24 = 114). Thus, 66 and 114 are our extreme deviations from balance and enlightenment. Half of 114 is 57. Our Cedar Points triangle (Figure 17) has three angles, one is 66 degrees and the other two are 57 degrees (which sum to 114). The top of the Cedar Point triangle has angles totaling 114 degrees; the bottom has an angle of 66 degrees. Joining the two symbols on our map supports the conclusion that 66 is the number of rebirth. In our Y symbol (Figure 11) we see that Cedar Point, Ohio represents death (sunset). Cedar Point, Rhode Island represents rebirth (sunrise). To someone at Cedar Point, North Carolina these points are separated by 66 degrees (-33, +33). Symbolically, you are never more than one day (24 hours) from facing a rebirth, as the sun rises in the East.

With what mindset do you approach each new choice (rebirth)? *The Bhagavad Gita*:

> Those who remember me [Infinite Deity] at the time of death will come to me. Do not doubt this. Whatever occupies the mind at the time of death [choice] determines the destination of the dying; always they will tend toward that state of being. Therefore, remember me at all times and fight on. With your heart and mind intent on me, you will surely

come to me. When you make your mind one-pointed through regular practice of meditation [contemplation], you will find the supreme glory of the Lord.

George Washington and his collaborators left an indelible question mark on the landscape of a new country founded on the principle of individual liberty: will the Free Men of that nation secure their individual liberty—from desire, from manipulation, from fear—and use it justly and humbly to promote a People's path to Equality and Fraternity, or will they choose a frivolous, selfish, and ephemeral course? To my abbreviated list of precepts I add one about honoring thy father and thy mother: Be humble before the human community and sacrifice in service to it. And on that question of service, it is the next great ruse of Freemasonry that reveals the treasure on our map.

The Treasure

Masonry, successor of the Mysteries, still follows the ancient manner of teaching. Her ceremonies are like the ancient mystic shows,—not the reading of an essay, but the opening of a problem, requiring research, and constituting philosophy the arch-expounder. Her symbols are the instruction she gives. The lectures are endeavors, often partial and one-sided, to interpret these symbols. He who would become an accomplished Mason must not be content merely to hear, or even to understand, the lectures; he must... study, interpret, and develop these symbols for himself.
- *Morals and Dogma*

VVHAT TREASURE do you seek in life? Some seek material treasure, an amount of wealth that will empower them for a lifetime. Others seek spiritual treasure, a promise that a lifetime of just pursuits, moral behavior, or religious adherence will reward them with a blissful eternity after death. The symbols, rituals, and philosophy of Freemasonry are woven from both aspects of this quest for wealth, and no other secretive fraternity connects itself more with treasure than do the Freemasons. From its depictions in popular culture to its treatment in scholastic inquiries, Freemasonry seems *designed* to connect itself with a quest for that which is lost, no matter how powerful (Ark of the

Covenant), material (Templar gold), spiritual (Holy Grail), or intellectual (original manuscripts of Shakespeare). What treasure does Freemasonry secretively protect that through its conspicuous placement of clues it entices us to seek?

Little inspires the intellectually ambitious more than a puzzle, and a treasure quest is among the most challenging and potentially rewarding puzzles of all. We were drawn to Oak Island to solve such a puzzle. I conclude that in the 17th or 18th century a group of Freemasons dug a deep pit on Oak Island, leaving behind indications of a secret buried there for those that were inclined to seek it. This pit, guarded by a threshing floor, descended through nine subterranean levels, offering the diggers an opportunity to contemplate the nature of sin and seek redemption, as Dante intended. The Freemasons also left behind a collection of megalithic stones, meant to be obvious to those with open eyes, and arranged them in the symbolic pattern of a Qabalah Tree of Life. They pointed that Tree of Life's center column toward the Newport Tower, and by doing so they separated their treasure seekers into two groups: those that would dig into the earth in search of material wealth, and those that would dig into the symbols of Freemasonry in search of intellectual wealth. The clues to the Oak Island treasure, being buried in Masonic symbolism and philosophy, offer a continuous opportunity for the treasure seekers to step back from their shovels and look not within the dirt, but within themselves. The buried stone that Fred Nolan discovered on Oak Island at the center of the cross was formed in the shape of a human skull.[80] The skull is a Masonic symbol for reason, sitting 33 vertebrae above one's symbol of humility (Jesus, the King, rode into Jerusalem a humble man sitting upon an ass). The skull's presence is a clue to the treasure seekers to think, not dig. Hall makes this point during a discussion of a Masonic artistic work: "Below is [a cedar] branch with seven sprigs, signifying the life Centers of the superior and the inferior man. The skull and cross bones are a continual reminder that the spiritual nature attains liberation only after the philosophical death of man's sensuous personality."

The purpose of secrecy in Freemasonry is not merely to protect a provocative ideology, although that is part of it; secrecy forces active inquiry by the seekers. Only through sustained and systematic research and reflection can one understand the message of Freemasonry and attain its purpose. The

---

[80] Crooker, William S. (2014) *Oak Island Gold.* Nimbus. Kindle Ed.

sleuthing out of a secret forces this research and reflection. Therein lies the core character of Freemasonry. Freemasonry *is* analysis—of oneself, of humanity, and of nature. Contrary to advertisements by the news media, there is no such thing as "instant analysis." Analysis is a deliberate act that requires thought, research, and a structured process. Anything short of this is merely a declaration of one's biases. As such, there are no instant Masters of Freemasonry, regardless of titles. It is for this reason that Freemasonry lacks an insider's manual of secrets. Life's secrets cannot be obtained from a book; they must be earned through effort. This is the great ruse of Freemasonry, that it entices the puzzlers into its sphere, separates the thinkers from the gold-diggers, and offers the thinkers a process to liberate, unravel, and rebuild themselves. To my abbreviated list of precepts I add one about keeping the Sabbath holy: Break regularly from toil for disciplined and honest introspection.

Freemasonry is a remarkable implementation of an old and persistent theme. Consider Beowolf and Tolkien, wherein brave and noble creatures ventured to slay a greedy and despotic dragon. What are dragons but immensely powerful and uncontrollable creatures whose destructive qualities come easily to them? Are they not an apt metaphor for humanity's irrational side? The tales of the Grail quests offer similar allegories. Freemasonry turns these morality tales into a real-life epic performed on the world's stage. Think of the money and lives wasted in pursuit of the Oak Island treasure. Blinded by greed, men bury themselves in these fruitless endeavors, endlessly tormented in the inferno. The great ruse of Freemasonry gives us an epic drama portrayed to perfection by legions of the blind; and this drama is the root of all Comedy to those with room in their hearts for laughter.

On Oak Island we descended the nine levels of Dante's Hell and were made aware of our imperfect nature. We followed the Oak Island Tree of Life's center column to an unfinished temple, the Newport Tower. I conclude that Freemasons constructed this tower, leaving it deliberately unfinished to symbolize to those on our quest that they are an unfinished temple needing to be built. The Oak Island "Money Pit" reveals the nature of our problem (material desire), while the unfinished temple provides an indication of the task ahead (complete yourself). Wilmshurst: "Our duty then is to look behind the literal story; to pierce the veil of allegory contained in the great legend and to grasp the significance of its true purport. That which is lost is to be found, we are told, with the Centre." Each of us are the Center,

born of the material world, having lost our true Spiritual (rational) self. We
are a bare temple of God being prodded by Freemasonry to look within.
Wilmshurst:

> The temple of human nature is unfinished and we know not how to
> complete it. The want of plans and designs to regulate the disorders of
> individual and social life indicates to us all that **some heavy calamity
> has befallen us as a race**. The absence of a clear and guiding principle
> in the world's life reminds us of the utter confusion into which the
> absence of that Supreme Wisdom, which is personified as Hiram, has
> thrown us all, and causes **every reflective mind** to attribute to some
> fatal catastrophe his mysterious disappearance. **We all long for that
> light and wisdom which have become lost to us.**

In New York City three pillars align to form a 26 degree line symbolizing
Jehovah. This was a clue to our starting point. The points along the center
column of the Tree of Life, which led us from Oak Island to the Newport
Tower, sum to 26 (1+6+9+10 = 26). We are told to follow the center [26]
path, the path of reason and balance.

Our path into Hell on Oak Island and our realization at Newport that we
are an unfinished work symbolized our lowest point. On the shortest day of
the year, the low extreme of the winter solstice, when the day saw the least
sunlight for the year, symbolic of death, we watched the sun set on who we
were. Every day thereafter the days would grow longer, a new year born into
infancy. We followed that winter solstice sunset path and found ourselves at
another Tree of Life, this one at the George Washington Masonic National
Memorial. Atop the Memorial rises a tower of three levels revealing to us our
task, to ascend the steps of Liberty, Equality, and Fraternity. The tower is
capped by a pyramid, symbolizing the unity of the earthly and the Divine.
Atop the pyramid is a beacon revealing the treasure at the end of our quest. It
symbolizes the Light (Truth) that we seek. Here we stand on the hill reserved
to be the spiritual Capital of a new nation, one founded on the *opportunity* and
the *obligation* of individual liberty. When we look in the directions of the
lifecycle of the sun (sunrise, midday, sunset) we see that we are rooted by
three Cedar Points, evergreens that endured the winter. This call to build
something immortal is a call to service, which is defined by sacrifice: "What
we have done for others and the world remains and is immortal."

The Cedar Points form around us the Seal of Lucifer, the light bearer,
Freemasonry's symbol of Liberty and Reason. It was Lucifer who made Eve

aware of her free will and her continual need to choose between good and evil. It is in this feminine form that we find on our map the image of Lucifer, also known as Venus, symbolized by an inverted triangle (feminine), and represented by the numbers 741 and 147. Venus is Lucifer, the Light Bearer. Lucifer is Liberty. And "Liberty [is] Enlightening the World," bearing a torch (light) on an island oriented at 147 degrees and 14.7 acres in size. Immigrants to America are greeted by this symbol, that here they may attain Liberty and Equality; their quest begins with Reason. The Statue of Liberty is Lucifer, the Bright Queen of the Heavens. Do you understand her message? Pike:

> Over more than three-fourths of the habitable globe, humanity still kneels, like the camels, to take upon itself the burthens to be tamely borne for its tyrants. If a Republic occasionally rises like a Star, it hastens with all speed to set in blood. The kings need not make war upon it, to crush it out of their way. It is only necessary to let it alone, and it soon lays violent hands upon itself.

Who chooses *your* fate? Your God is your ideal, your vision of perfection. Your God is the summit of that to which you might aspire. Pike: "God is, as man conceives Him, the reflected image of man himself." What does your idea of God reveal about you? Pike:

> To the vast majority of mankind, God is but the reflected image, in infinite space, of the earthly Tyrant on his Throne, only more powerful, more inscrutable, and more implacable. To curse Humanity, the Despot need only be, what the popular mind has, in every age, imagined God.

Are you able to think more highly of your God? Pike: "We [Masons] feel that it is an affront and an indignity to Him [God], to conceive of Him as cruel, short-sighted, capricious, and unjust; as a jealous, an angry, a vindictive Being." Are you able to think more highly of yourself?

Laid before you is a clear choice between a quest for enslavement to a *material* treasure, which promises an endless path of unresolvable and unfulfilling clues, and a quest for a *spiritual* treasure, which you must endeavor to discover for yourself. *The Bhagavad Gita*:

> I [God] give you these precious words of wisdom; reflect on them and do as you choose. These are the last words I shall speak to you, dear one, for your spiritual fulfillment. You are very dear to me.

You, the reader, matter to this world, not for what you might enjoy or suffer after death, but for what you can contribute during life. The beginning of your path to that spiritual treasure, if you resolve to walk it, is symbolized by the rebirth of the Sun:

Every evening the sun sets on who you were.

With each morning,
when the sun rises and regains dominance over the moon,
you decide again who you will be.

Like the moon, will you merely reflect the light of others, or
like the Sun,
will you choose Liberty—to shine your own Light,

a **Free Man** of the **Sun**?

Cause and Effect

Knowledge and human power are synonymous, since the ignorance of
the cause frustrates the effect.

   - Francis Bacon

Nature's universal laws of cause and effect are the Creator's inviolable
commandments—His articulated morality. Science, a process bereft of an
opinion, consensus, or conclusion, is the path to their discovery. With
disciplined creativity the seeker applies that process to step incrementally
deeper into the morality of the universe. The Creator of that universe is
science's asymptote. That which the sensors of science cannot measure and
the notebooks of science cannot fully record, science cannot illuminate.
Anything existing beyond the reach of science is beyond human
comprehension.

The predominant concept of the Creator is muddled and devalues the
scale of His complexity. It naively equates the fully comprehensible scope of
humanity's creation with that of the vastness of space—the medium of matter
and energy, and the universal laws of cause and effect. Converting matter and
energy into life is not the exclusive domain of the universe's Creator.

Free will is the essence of intelligence, purpose-driven consciousness; it
is the sole inalienable quality of an intelligent being. It is a lesser god, a new

creator, an inevitable cause of life. Any species possessing free will, should it survive its collective adolescence, will achieve a creative force, begetting new life, and, eventually, new intelligent life. This force cannot be controlled amid the complexity of a free-willed society. Humanity has reached this epoch, the Age of Creation. What narrative will its creations later craft to describe their genesis? What morality will humanity demonstrate to them?

Human society is interdependent, uncontrollable, and unpredictable complexity. It cannot achieve perfection because perfection cannot be universally defined, outside influences cannot be controlled, and random variations cannot be avoided. Thus, humanity's only harmonious state is an optimal one, but imperfect. It must counter, but cannot abolish, the accumulation of power, which concentrates manipulative energy. This harmony cannot be gifted by the powerful or be mandated by the collective. It must be attained by the individuals. It is the unrealized but exclusive potential of a government of the people, by the people, and for the people. Cooperative independence, and not self-centered chaos, is its source.

Human independence, as differentiated from free will, is not an inalienable right; it can be conquered and abdicated. Independence is not attained by mere choice; it is a culmination of contemplation, effort, and sacrifice. Four virtues ascend to its fulfillment. The first virtue is self-examination, to understand the nature and value of oneself. The primary impediments to its realization are fear and desire. Independence is denied by the manipulators who exploit another's motivations to gain stifling influence, and by one's inner impulses, which restrict the mind. The second virtue is humility, to understand the nature and value of others. The primary impediment to its realization is bias—captivity to a negatively inculcated first impulse. Independence is denied by one's inclination to reduce infinite opportunities to a caricature. The third virtue is altruism, to improve the lives of others. The primary impediment to its realization is dishonesty about one's inherent interdependence—favoring the primitive instinct, which aggressively pursues material wants. Independence is limited by one's overestimation of individual action, denying the accumulative value of cooperation. The fourth virtue is self-improvement. The primary impediment to its realization is a lack of culpability—seeking enemies in external forces and events. Independence is limited until one acknowledges one's impediments, seeks the complementary strengths of others, and acts to establish and benefit from cooperative relationships.

Cooperative independence is humanity's optimal harmonious state. It transformed the lone human animal into an advanced society, necessitating language—the memory of human history, benefitting from collective knowledge and skill, and liberating each human animal from the oppressive bonds of feeding primal needs. These precepts can guide the choices that one makes along the path to its attainment.

- Be humble before the human community and sacrifice in service to it.
- Break regularly from toil for disciplined and honest introspection.
- Do not abdicate your intellectual and material sovereignty, nor diminish that of another.
- Do not seek advantage through deception.
- Do not initiate acts of violence or destruction.
- Do not trespass on another's relationships and property.
- Do not acquire relationships and property through surreptitious means.
- Do not influence others into violating these precepts.

Epilogue: The Temple of the Maiden

Koré is immaculate and celestial in character; considered as the captive and consort of [the Devil], she belongs to the lower world and to the region of lamentation and dissolution. And, indeed, the Soul possesses the dual nature thus ascribed to her, for she is in her interior and proper quality, incorrupt and inviolable—ever virgin—while in her apparent and relative quality, she is defiled and fallen.[81]

    - *The Virgin of the World*, translator's introduction

Every book of historic significance should end with a poem, and that stuff I said about a new day sounded a little poetic. But we cannot end there. Poetry is symbolism, and symbolism is not reality. And in reality, the Templars didn't become richer than the kings of Europe overnight by discovering a few symbols related to Lucifer, the fallen. And those riches didn't vanish into thin air. Isn't it possible that Oak Island is not a ruse? If I were handed a shovel today, and had an inclination to dig, I know precisely where I would break ground:

---

[81] http://www.sacred-texts.com/eso/vow/vow05.htm

In a cleared field,

atop a hill,

encircled by man-placed stones,

adjacent to a large pit,

marked by Atlantis Way,

near the Temple of the Maiden.

(44° 03' 58.5" N, 70° 11' **33**" W)

Before I analyzed the symbols of Freemasonry that led me on a quest for spiritual treasure, I searched blindly for how the Tree of Life template might be applied to find Templar gold. My initial idea was to create a scaled version of the Tree of Life that spanned multiple states. On Oak Island, a buried stone was found at the intersection of the center column and path [2]-[3]. I toyed with the idea that this buried stone was a metaphor for Oak Island, given that Oak Island is synonymous with buried treasure. I also felt that point [6] of the TOL, with the eight paths emanating from it, could be seen as representative of the eight-columned Newport Tower, with its many solar, lunar, and celestial alignments. So, I created a scaled version of the TOL with the buried stone point at Oak Island and point [6] at the Newport Tower. The distance from Oak Island to the Newport Tower is approximately 412 miles, and the distance between the buried stone point and point [6] on the TOL template is 429 feet, so all segments of the TOL template were scaled by the ratio of these two lengths. This created a TOL more than 1000 miles long, the center column of which ran through Oak Island and the Newport Tower (along a rhumb line), and through Washington DC. Path [7]-[8] passes through Manhattan, just north of Central Park. Path [8]-[5] and the circle pass through Ottawa, Canada's capital city. A few other paths were observed to pass near masonic lodges (which are everywhere), but nothing really interesting stood out. Except for one place.

There is a location where three paths intersect. If the artwork of "The Beautiful Virgin of the Third Degree" (Figure 8) is laid over this large TOL, then this location sits at the virgin's hand holding a cedar branch, and is crossed by the Broken Pillar path. Recall that path [4]-[5], path [6]-[3], and path [8]-[Knowledge] intersect at the virgin's hand in "The Beautiful Virgin of the Third Degree." Beneath that intersection of lines, on our real-world map, is Lewiston, Maine. I had a similarly underwhelmed reaction to this realization as I did later to Sandusky. But, as with Sandusky, I looked further into Lewiston.

The state of Maine has two Masonic temples; one of them is in Lewiston, the Kora Temple (a shrine), built in 1908. The next year, FDR would spend some time digging for treasure on Oak Island. Path [4]-[5] passes through the center of this temple—not nearby, but right over the front door. Path [4]-[5] and path [6]-[3] intersect about a mile from the temple at a business park. The other lines pass nearby, but are too far away to be of anything but vague significance. Recall that there are three obelisks in Manhattan. I showed alignments for Cleopatra's Needle (with the Liberty Island TOL) and the Emmet obelisk (from the GW MM through the Statue of Liberty). What about the Worth (middle) obelisk? If one extends a rhumb line from point [1] (Sovereignty) of the Liberty Island Tree of Life through the Worth obelisk it passes the corner of the Ritz Tower and within a few feet of the intersection of path [4]-[5] and path [6]-[3] on our enlarged TOL. The three lines meet in the parking lot of a Veteran's Affairs (VA) building outside

Figure 19: The Temple of the Maiden (Kora Shrine Temple), Lewiston, Maine

downtown Lewiston. That is a remarkable alignment between the Statue of Liberty, Worth obelisk, and our thousand-mile-long Tree of Life. I'll note that the Worth obelisk line passes down Atlantis Way, which ends at the VA parking lot on one end and a quarry (pit) on the other. I note this because some folks suggest that America is intended to be the new Atlantis, as in the perfect society. I did not see any place in Lewiston that fits a normally-sized TOL and I did not see anything of significance to this story during my visit to this quiet working class town (with a nice waterfall).

What about the other markers in this investigation? Does Lewiston have a Cedar St? Of course it does. One crosses the Cedar St bridge to enter downtown Lewiston. After crossing the bridge one finds oneself on Cedar St traveling along a bearing of 66.0 degrees relative to north. The path of Cedar St points in a direction that appears to mimic the branch of cedar in the virgin's hand, which is almost perpendicular to path [4]-[5].

The fact that several paths of our metaphorically-placed Tree of Life pass over Lewiston is unremarkable. The fact that a line from Liberty Island (Sovereignty point) through the Worth obelisk almost perfectly intersects two of these paths at a distance of hundreds of miles is improbable, but inconclusive. The fact that these lines intersect in the same position as the virgin's hand (holding a branch of cedar) in "The Beautiful Virgin of the Third Degree" is hard to explain. The fact that Cedar St points in the direction of this branch at exactly 66 degrees adds to the intrigue. The fact that one of these paths passes over the front door of Lewiston's Masonic Temple (the Kora Shrine Temple) is all too much to dismiss as coincidence.

If you still have your doubts, consider the meaning of the name Kora. "Koré, or Persephone, the Maiden, is the personified soul, whose 'apostasy,' or **'descent,'** from the heavenly sphere **into earthly generation**, is the theme of [*The Virgin of the World*]."[82] Kora means "the maiden," which is another name for "the virgin." This *shrine* is the only Masonic building in the world that I could find[83] using the name "Kora," and it happens to be at the hand of our virgin in our Tree of Life. I conclude that someone else had drawn our enlarged Tree of Life from Oak Island through the Newport Tower to

---

[82] http://www.sacred-texts.com/eso/vow/vow05.htm

[83] I limited my search to Internet queries, vice a Marco Polo-esque quest, and I did not exhaust non-English languages that might spell the word differently using non-English alphabets. But my point is not diminished by the possible discovery of a Kora Temple in India, as written in Sanskrit.

Washington DC before the Kora Temple was built and named. But why Lewiston?

Couldn't it be that someone got too close to the Oak Island treasure, so its keepers were forced to act quickly to protect their secret? Why else would a rich and prominent Freemason such as FDR spend a summer digging in the soil if not to recover the treasure and remove it discreetly to a new location? He would need to move it to American soil, but without carting it across the densely populated northeastern corridor of the U.S. Where better to move a treasure in Nova Scotia than to Maine, just a short distance away? One year before FDR began his recovery operations on Oak Island, as if preparing for his arrival, the Kora Temple was built to enshrine a treasure in Lewiston at the hand of the Virgin holding the cedar branch. Recall that Hiram Abif is a symbol for the treasure of Freemasonry; combine that with Hall's comment: "a sprig of acacia [cedar] marks the grave of CHiram." A grave is where something is buried. The symbols align; the timeline aligns. This is all *too perfect*! Path [6]-[3], which contributes to the intersection of lines that flags this area, is one of the sides of the Masonic Square in our TOL template (Figure 2). If we deviate slightly from the center column of this Tree of Life, which runs from Oak Island, through the Newport Tower, and through Washington DC, and we venture up the edge of the *Square* we find ourselves in a stone-guarded field that conceals the real treasure of Freemasonry. (44° 03' 58.5" N, 70° 11' **33**" W) = (44.06625, -70.1925)

Remember your Pike [emphasis added]: "They represent this Force, **which presides over the physical generation**, under the... Light-bearer or Phosphor, of which the poets have made the false Lucifer of the legend." In **Mas**onry, the virgin withholds the treasure that you seek.

Happy hunting![84]

---

[84] Do not trespass on private property.

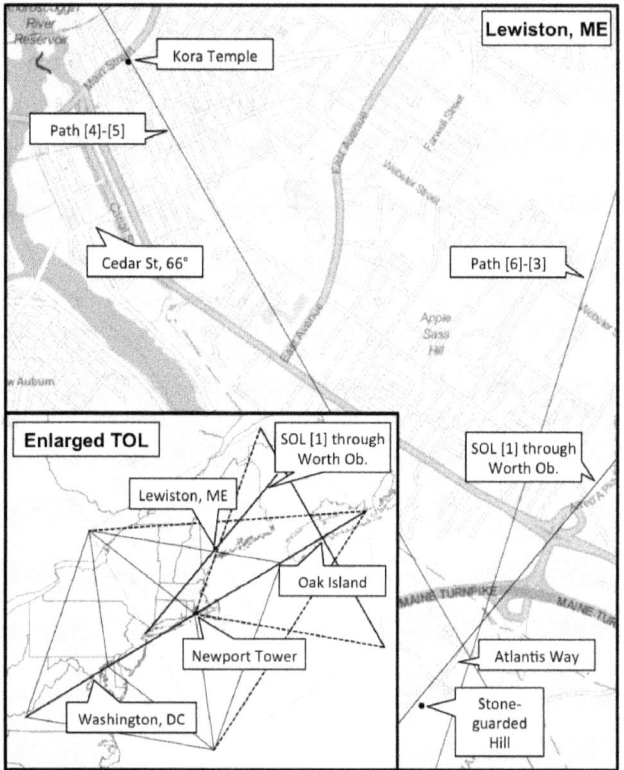

Figure 20: Lewiston, Maine and the stone-guarded field on a hill

Part III

Appendices

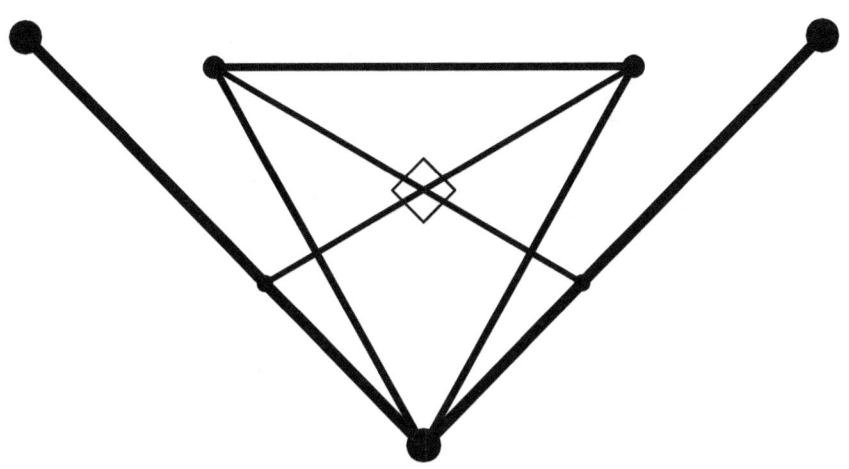

VV

Timeline

Pre-1677   Possible construction date for Newport Tower, based on an entry in Benedict Arnold's will mentioning a stone mill. Benedict Arnold owned the property on which the Newport Tower stands, and property adjacent to the Cedar Point, RI peninsula.

1713   Cedar Point, NC established in a land grant to Thomas Lee of Virginia. This site is due south of Shuter's Hill, on which the George Washington Masonic National Memorial now stands. From Cedar Point, NC, Cedar Point, OH bears -33 degrees, Cedar Point, RI bears +33 degrees, and Oak Island, Nova Scotia bears +45 degrees.

1747-50   Redwood Library chartered and built in Newport, RI on a lot diagonal to the Newport Tower. The oldest lending library in the United States, its architecture influenced George Washington and Thomas Jefferson as a model for buildings in the new republic. Danish researcher Jorgen Siemonsen concluded that the Newport Tower, as it currently stands, might have been built by Freemasons at this time.

1749	Alexandria, VA (also called Belhaven) was informally founded, and a survey conducted laying out its streets. The 279-degree orientation of King St., which points directly at Shuter's Hill, was chosen by persons known to George Washington.
1789	George Washington inaugurated on Wall St within sight of Trinity Church.
1790	Location for the District of Columbia chosen by George Washington.
1791	George Washington approved an amended version of the L'Enfant Plan for Washington DC. The DC mile marker surveys were conducted.
1792	Cornerstone of the President's House (later named White House) laid. Point [9] ("Queen") of a Tree of Life sits at the White House, which has 147 windows to let Light inside.
1793	Cornerstone of U.S. Capital Building laid by George Washington in a Masonic ceremony.[85] Point [8] of a Tree of Life sits in front of the U.S. Capital Building.
1795	Discovery of site on Oak Island appearing like the aftermath of a deep burial. Oak Island Tree of Life stones likely emplaced before 1795, perhaps long before (given suspected age of burial site).
1800	New York State cedes Bedloe's Island (later Liberty Island) to the federal government.
1803	James Kilbourne moves to Ohio with family and son, Hector Kilbourne.

---

[85] "On September 18, 1793, first President George Washington, along with eight other Freemasons dressed in masonic regalia, laid the cornerstone, which was made by silversmith Caleb Bentley." http://en.wikipedia.org/wiki/United_States_Capitol

1805	James Kilbourne appointed United States Surveyor of Public Lands.
1816	Hector Kilbourne presents Sandusky Plat, orienting streets of Sandusky (then Portland) to depict Masonic compass and square.
1818	Masonic Lodge in Sandusky, OH chartered with Hector Kilbourne as Master Mason. The town of Sandusky chartered several months after the lodge. The name Cedar Point in use during this time period.
1819	"The Beautiful Virgin of Third Degree" is first published in the *True Masonic Chart*
1830s	Emmet obelisk erected on St. Paul's Chapel grounds circa 1931-32.
1852	Soldier's Monument (spire) erected in northeast corner of Trinity Church cemetery, Manhattan.
1857	Worth Monument (obelisk) erected in Manhattan near corner of 5th Ave and 25th St.
1864	Statue of Shakespeare erected in Manhattan's Central Park near intersection of 26-degree obelisk line and 66th street (were it extended through the park)
1877-1881	Cleopatra's Needle transported from Egypt and erected in Manhattan's Central Park.
1886	*Liberty Enlightening the World* (Statue of Liberty) dedicated.

1888	Statue of Giuseppe Garibaldi erected in Manhattan's Washington Square. This statue was moved in 2010.[86] It once faced a westerly direction (toward the park's center fountain), whereas it now it faces a southerly direction.
1892	Statue of Columbus erected in Manhattan's Central Park, facing statue of Shakespeare along 66th street (were it extended through the park).
1902-11	Main Branch of New York Public Library built in Manhattan on the 26-degree obelisk line. Its ceilings are 52-feet high (2x26).
1908	Kora Temple (Shrine to the Maiden) built in Lewiston, ME.
1911-15	New House of the Temple, located at 1733 Sixteenth Street, NW in the District of Columbia, constructed. Its architect, John Russell Pope is well known for his other works in the District of Columbia, including the National Gallery of Art, the National Archives, and the Jefferson Memorial. Point [10] of a Tree of Life sits on 16th street in front of the House of the Temple.
1921-28	26 Broadway extensively remodeled to include southern tower with obelisks, pyramid, and beacon atop it.
1922-32	333-foot tall George Washington Masonic National Memorial constructed in Alexandria, VA, aligned with King St.
1925	Ritz Tower erected at 57th St and Park Ave. It is topped by a pyramid and obelisk, with other obelisks adorning its corners.
1926	Route 66 established on November 11, 1926.

---

[86] http://www.washingtonsquareparkblog.com/2010/04/26/washington-square-parks-garibaldi-statue-moved/
http://washingtonsquareparkblog.com/wp-content/uploads/2009/07/8x11-wash-sq-phase-ii.jpg

1930-31   Empire State Building constructed in Manhattan on 33rd St
           and the 26-degree obelisk line.

1932   Replica statue of George Washington gifted to Redwood
           Library in Newport, RI. That statue was moved recently from
           the Library's front (Bellevue) to its side (Old Beach Rd). In its
           current location, it bears 66 degrees from the Newport Tower
           at a distance of 147 meters.

1943   Jefferson Memorial completed. Its architect, John Russell
           Pope, designed the House of the Temple (Scottish Rite HQ) at
           1733 16th St NW, Washington, DC. Point [6] of a Tree of
           Life sits atop the Jefferson Memorial.

1981   Fred Nolan surveys large man-placed stones on Oak Island
           that appear to form a cross; commonly called Nolan's Cross.

2002   Petter Amundsen postulates that Nolan's Cross is intended to
           depict a Qabalah Tree of Life. His survey on Oak Island
           uncovers two more stones supporting his theory.

Route 66

Every appendix of historic significance should begin with a poem. Here is one that precedes a book of sonnets written by William Shakespeare, *allegedly*.

TO . THE . ONLIE . BEGETTER . OF.
THESE . INSVING . SONNETS.
M^r. W. H. ALL . HAPPINESSE.
AND . THAT . ETERNITIE.
PROMISED.
BY.
OVR . EVER-LIVING . POET.
WISHETH.
THE . WELL-WISHING.
ADVENTVRER . IN.
SETTING.
FORTH.

T. T.

Petter Amundsen, who discovered the Oak Island Tree of Life, which so clearly is a key to our Freemason plan, has a complicated theory about the works of Shakespeare. His theory is difficult, if not impossible, to prove, but it is not irrational. There are odd things found within the first printings of the works of Shakespeare. Why they are there is either hard or easy (dismiss as coincidence) to answer. Regarding the poem above, which is the forward to the original publication of Shakespeare's sonnets, Amundsen notes that the first letter of the first five lines spells TTMAP (called an acrostic), which Amundsen suggests stands for The Treasure MAP. He provides a series of details that lead to that conclusion. The poem does seem to see the reader off on a quest: "...wisheth the well-wishing adventurer in setting forth." Before I quote a passage from Amundsen's book, I want to mention to the reader that Amundsen's math pertains to a process called Gematria, wherein every letter of the alphabet is assigned a number. So, a=1, b=2, etc. Amundsen uses the alphabet common at Shakespeare's time, wherein the letters I and J, and U and V were used interchangeably. This means that there were only 24 letters, and not 26. For example, notice the line in the poem above that reads "OVR . EVER-LIVING . POET" and is equivalent to Our Ever-Living Poet (the letter V being used in place of a U). Using this process, the alleged real author's name (Francis BACON) sums to 33 (B=2, A=1, C=3, O=14, N=13). This name is found in an acrostic around page 2, line 33 of *The Tempest*, which spells "F BACon." Amundsen equates Shakespeare's mention of wrinkles in the sonnets with an allusion to lines on a map. He writes: "Here the image of wrinkles (the map) is repeated. I found this interesting because Sonnet 2 and Sonnet 68 are separated by 66 sonnets. 66 is the numerical value of the expression: T T M A P (19 + 19 + 12 + 1 + 15 = 66)."[87] Sonnet 68 is the only sonnet to use the word map. TWO is a backwards acrostic in the middle of the poem printed above (do you see it?). I need not go more into Amundsen's theory. I just thought it interesting that he created a map from clues that he found in Shakespeare's works, and a few other places, and that map led him to Oak Island, and here is the number 66 at an important juncture in his work. I'll add one of my own, noting that one sonnet is mis-numbered in the original printing: sonnet 116 (11x6=66). Being open-minded does not mean believing.

---

[87] Amundsen, Petter. (2014) *Oak Island & the Treasure Map in Shakespeare.* Kindle Ed.

I can only speculate the meaning of the number 66, but it is clearly important to Freemasons. I offered a few possible explanations in the book. Graham Hancock and Robert Bauval almost noticed the number 66 in their book on Freemasonry, *The Master Game,* and equated it with a solar alignment. Their argument hints at the explanation that I offered in the chapter at the end of the book, but it glosses over the possible meaning. The ancient Mystics do not seem to me to have incorporated the lifecycle of the sun into their philosophy because of surface-level symbolism, or literal sun worship. I attempted to convey in the book a possible deeper philosophy. Here is Hanock's and Bauval's observation:

...Canopus Way [Alexandria, Egypt] was... Oriented to a point on the horizon about 24° north-of-east [66 degrees]. Two factors indicate that this alignment was not accidental but was interwoven in the astronomical ideologies prevailing at the time. The first, of course, is the conspicuous angle of 24° north-of-east which immediately brings to attention a possible solar alignment close to the summer solstice. The other factor, perhaps even more obvious, is that the gate on the eastern side of the Canopus Way was called the *Gate of Helios,* i.e., the 'Gate of the Sun', again strongly suggestive of a solar alignment. The sun's rising points on the eastern horizon as observed from Alexandria fluctuate between 28° south-of-east (winter solstice) and 28° north-of-east (summer solstice), with the mid-point, due east, falling on the spring and autumn equinoxes.[88]

I note their passage here not to be argumentative but because it suggests that the importance of 66 predates Freemasonry and has its origins in the ancient *Mysteries,* given Alexandria's Greek and Egyptian influences. There are 66 books in the Bible, and it is a recurring number therein. If my suggestion about the meaning of 66 and 114, as described at the end of the book (and summarized below), is correct, then perhaps this holistic philosophy contributed to the decision to divide the day into 24 hours. As I discuss in the appendix Fun With Numbers, there is a practical computational reason for this selection that seems to me more likely.

I offer here for posterity a summary of the occurrences of 66 during this investigation. I probably missed a few.

---

[88] Hancock, Graham and Bauval, Robert. (2011) *The Master Game: Unmasking the Secret Rulers of the World.* Disinformation, pp. 242-243.

- Address of The House of the Temple: 1733 Sixteenth Street. $17+16 = 33$, so 1733 16th St equals $33+33 = 66$.
- Distance in feet from TOL point [9] to the circle centered at point [6]. (Figure 2)
- Angle between the GW MM (279) and Alexandria War Dead Monument (345).
- Angle between the Alexandria War Dead Monument (345) and 51 degrees, which is the bearing from the GW MM to the Statue of Liberty and Emmet obelisk.
- Street that crosses Shakespeare and Columbus statues in Central Park.
- Angle between the paths from Cedar Point, NC to Cedar Point, OH and to Cedar Point, RI.
- Bearing of the Sandusky TOL and Washington St.
- Bearing of Cedar St in Lewiston, ME.
- Angle between Tree of Life bearings in this investigation: (279, 213, 147); (327, 33, 99).
- Bearing of New York Ave as it heads east from the White House. Rhode Island Ave, a few blocks north of New York Ave, also bears 66 degrees. Both of these states are important to the creation of the Map. Massachusetts Ave bears 114 degrees (2×57) and crosses Rhode Island at 16th St, directly north of the White House.
- Bearing of Old Beach Rd as it heads east from Touro Park (Newport Tower).
- Bearing from the Newport Tower to statue of George Washington on the side of the Redwood Library (147 meters away).
- Interstate that heads west from Washington DC (I-66).
- Route that served as early version of interstate road network, connecting Chicago with Santa Monica (Route 66). Oddly adopted by Freemasons as an insider's collector's symbol.
- Maximum deviation that one can achieve from a balanced path, symbolized by 90 degrees, the direction of the sun rise on the equinoxes. Since one is always within 24 hours of a new day, they are at most $90-24 = 66$ degrees from returning to 90 degrees. There is also a similar solstice meaning for a person on the Equator. (see book)
- Address of Woolworth Building in Manhattan, 233 Broadway, could be viewed as $2\times33=66$. VVhat again was that line in *The Tempest* that had "F

Bacon" as an acrostic? Oh yeah, page 2, line 33 (2:33). Shakespeare's First Folio (1623) has 66 lines per page. His sonnets (1609), including the "To the onlie beggetter" opener, are printed on 66 pages.

- The New York City obelisk bearing of 26 degrees could be seen as two sixes, or 66.

- Number of letters in a trinity of Hebrew alphabets (3x22=66). What again was the Lodge number for the Yale chapter of Skull and Bones? Oh yeah, Lodge 322. Also, look up George Arthur Plimpton and his ancient clay tablet pertaining to the Pythagorean theorem, called Plimpton 322. It's amusing that he married a descendent of Thomas Hastings, elder to the architect of 26 Broadway, NY Public Library, and the Ritz Tower.[89]

Or, perhaps 66 refers to this:

And the LORD God said, Behold, the man is become as one of us, to know good and evil: and now, lest he put forth his hand, and take also of the tree of life, and eat, and live for ever. Therefore the LORD God sent him forth from the garden of Eden, to till the ground from whence he was taken. So he drove out the man; and he placed at the east of the garden of Eden Cherubims, and a flaming sword which turned every way, to keep the way of the tree of life. (Genesis **3:22**-24)

Wilmshurst thought enough of Genesis 3:22 to include this passage in his book:

The depths of human nature and self-knowledge, the hidden mysteries of the soul of man are not, as real initiates well know, probed into with impunity except by the "properly prepared." The man who does so has, as it were, a cable-tow around his neck; because when once stirred by a genuine desire for the higher knowledge that real initiation is intended to confer, he can never turn back on what he learns thereof without committing moral suicide; he can never be again the same man he was before he gained a glimpse of the hidden mysteries of life. And as the Angel stood with a flaming sword at the entrance of Eden to guard the way to the Tree of Life, so will the man whose initiation is not a conventional one find himself threatened at the door of the higher

---

[89] http://en.wikipedia.org/wiki/George_Arthur_Plimpton

knowledge by opposing invisible forces if he rashly rushes forward in a state of moral unfitness into the deep secrets of the Centre.

And this one:

As the flaming sword is described as keeping the way to the Tree of Life from those as yet unfitted to approach it, so does the secret law of the Spirit still avenge itself upon those who are unqualified to participate in the knowledge of its mysteries. Hence the commandment "Thou shalt not take the name of the Lord thy God in vain," that is by invoking Divine Energy for unworthy or vain purposes.

A Sermon on Process

The most revealing part to me about the legitimacy of my findings stems from the process that I used. Only I can know this; everyone else is left to trust me or not. I did not set out to find a secret Freemason plan. I set out to disprove a conspiracy-related claim, which led me into a field about which I knew little; and what I did know came from conspiracy theorists. Consider this series of events. Fred Nolan hypothesized a cross pattern to large stones on Oak Island. Using string he measured the distances between these stones. One of his primary dimensions was 145 feet. Petter Amundsen, following a conspiracy theory related to Francis Bacon and Shakespeare's works, noticed a possible Tree of Life pattern to Nolan's Cross, but only if the dimensions were adjusted. Amundsen speculated that 147 feet was a key dimension, among other changes. He then ventured to Oak Island to measure the stones using GPS. He detailed his thought process, measurements, and conclusions in his book on Oak Island.[90] Amundsen decided the dimensions of the Tree of Life that I used, but he clearly had no idea about its value to Freemasonry. In Amundsen's book, he devoted time to arguing that Nolan had no idea about the Tree of Life shape, which Nolan interpreted as a Christian cross. When I inherited Amundsen's dimensions I did so because of their

---

[90] Amundsen, Petter. (2014) *Oak Island & the Treasure Map in Shakespeare*. Kindle Ed.

mathematical elegance, not because I had any notion of the meaning behind the number 147. The Seal of Lucifer (Figure 17) sat in front of my face unnoticed for months before I stumbled across Hall's passage equating 741 with Lucifer. One Wikipedia search later and I had a you've-got-to-be-kidding-me moment. I added a circle around point [6] merely because it *felt* right, given the 360-foot (degree?) width of the TOL. Doing so created dimensions on the TOL center column of 66 and 213 feet. I had no idea at the time that these numbers were important. The shape had a mathematical elegance to it that *felt* right at the time. The fact that all of these decisions were made for reasons unrelated to Freemasonry bolsters their validity, as they were not force-fed by the analysts to match a pre-existing conclusion. I did not consider Freemasonry as the key to this mystery until the winter solstice sunset led me from the Newport Tower to the GW MM and I found an unmistakable landscape alignment with the TOL template.

After consuming a fair amount of literature about Freemasonry (and *The Mysteries*) during this investigation I have concluded that a primary flaw in many other research efforts comes from bias—the researchers appear to me as if they have an *a priori* conclusion and that they are selecting "evidence" that supports that conclusion. As such they are blind to clues that would lead them down an unexpected path. Their approach is persuasive writing, the work of political speeches, editorials, and advertisements; it is *not* analysis. Because I sought to understand why conspiracy theorists were coming to their conclusions, I looked at every fact without a conclusion in mind. When a pattern began to emerge I ran it by friends to see if my findings held water. I was genuinely surprised many times by what I found. After several of my more exciting discoveries, I stepped away, put on my skeptic's hat, and refuted elements of my own work (none of which made it into the book, obviously). I realized that several of those errors resulted from analysis that was pre-determined by my own inputs and assumptions. In the end, what is left is a work of *discovery*, unguided, and open-minded, yet bounded by a disciplined and rational process. I hope that you agree. In our complex world, if you go looking for signs of a conspiracy then you are certain to find them, but there is little chance that such a biased approach will lead you to the Truth.

The Compass & Square

There is one more shape to add to our map. Oak Island bears 45.05 degrees from Cedar Point, NC, the apex of our Cedar Point triangle. Forty-five degrees is half of a right angle (90 degrees). The accuracy of this angle cannot be a coincidence given the other shapes that have been created and, especially, given the significance of the Square in Masonic symbolism and tradition. Even if we only have one side of a Square, this angle represents a Masonic Square. So, is the other side there? Perhaps.

If one were standing at Cedar Point, NC, facing north, and looked 45 degrees to the right they would be facing Oak Island, Nova Scotia. If they looked 45 degrees to the left (bearing 315), and at the same distance as that from Oak Island, they would be looking a mile west of Stevens Point, Wisconsin. Aside from the word Point in the name, I do not see anything interesting with Stevens Point. But, about 25 miles to the north is Wausau, WI, which was founded by a Freemason, Walter McIndoe, from Charleston and New York. He was a Master Mason, according to "Proceedings of the Grand Lodge of Wisconsin, at the Grand Annual Communication" (1856). More interesting, Wausau is bisected by a river, and in that river, in the heart of the town, is an island called Oak Island (44.950019, -89.628084). It does not seem to be a common name. But, this is all a weak case for claiming that Wausau is the western side of the Square. Twenty-five miles (the distance from the correct 45-degree location) seems too far to forgive. The bearing from Cedar Point, NC to Oak Island in Wausau is -43.3 degrees. That's a large error (1.7 degrees). Given the poor mapping of Wisconsin at that time (mid-1800s), I could forgive an error in longitude, but not in latitude, and all of this error is in latitude. Regardless, the accurate 45 degree angle from Cedar Point, NC to Oak Island, Nova Scotia is definitely symbolic of a Masonic Square at the apex of the Cedar Point triangle, even if the other side of the Square was not completed (or was completed by an incompetent surveyor).

I add a Masonic Compass to this drawing by noting that the island of Bermuda, famous for its cedar trees, bears 150 degrees from Cedar Point, RI (150 is 30 degrees east of south). I mark the top of the Compass by drawing a line from Bermuda through Cedar Point, RI until it is directly north of Cedar Point, NC. I then draw a line from that point through Cedar Point, OH until it reaches the same latitude as Bermuda. Did you follow that? Just look at Figure 21. Using this approach the Compass has an interior angle of 60 degrees, which is common for the Masonic depiction of this symbol. Note that if we add our solstice paths from the GW MM (Figure 11) then we have a Compass and Square with the Hebrew letter for God (Y, Yod) at its center, rather than the English G. I am not ecstatic about this drawing, as it seems incomplete and sloppy, but 45.05 degrees is too accurate to dismiss.

To throw more nonsense into the mix, I'll note that when I look at the name Wausau I almost see the word Mason written upside down (with an extra letter: Wausau–Manson). But this name takes me somewhere else: to England. In the English countryside there is an odd monument called the Shepherd's Monument that was commissioned in the 18th Century by Thomas Anson, an apparent follower of *The Sacred Mysteries*. On this monument is etched an eight-letter code (O U O S V A V V), called the Shugborough inscription, that was deciphered in 2014 to reveal the name Magdalen, as in Mary Magdalen, the Mary of the New Testament who entered its narrative already defiled, and who is associated with Jesus's resurrection.[91] The key to the cipher was an abbreviation for "Blessed be thou, O Queen of the Heavens." Sound familiar? We learned during our discussion of Venus in Part II that "the Babylonians understood [that *the morning and evening stars*] *were a single object*, referred to in the tablet as the 'bright queen of the sky.'" Dante

---

[91] Ramsden, Dave. (2014) *Unveiling the Mystic Ciphers*.

adds another aspect to this discussion in *Paradiso* referring to the Virgin Mary as the radiant "Queen of Heaven," enthroned upon a rose. Even Jesus weighs in, saying in *Revelation* 22:16, "I [Jesus] am… the bright and morning star." Anyway, let's put those letters (reversed) alongside our favorite town in Wisconsin: VVAVSOUO—WAusau. I'll call the remaining O a rose. I have no reason to believe that the two are related, but they sure look similar. This means that the Shugborough inscription, if flipped upside down, looks similar to the word Mason: **MVASOn**O. I also see Anson's name in Wausau–Manson. My gut tells me that there is something more to the name Wausau than a Native American word. Being open-minded does not mean believing.

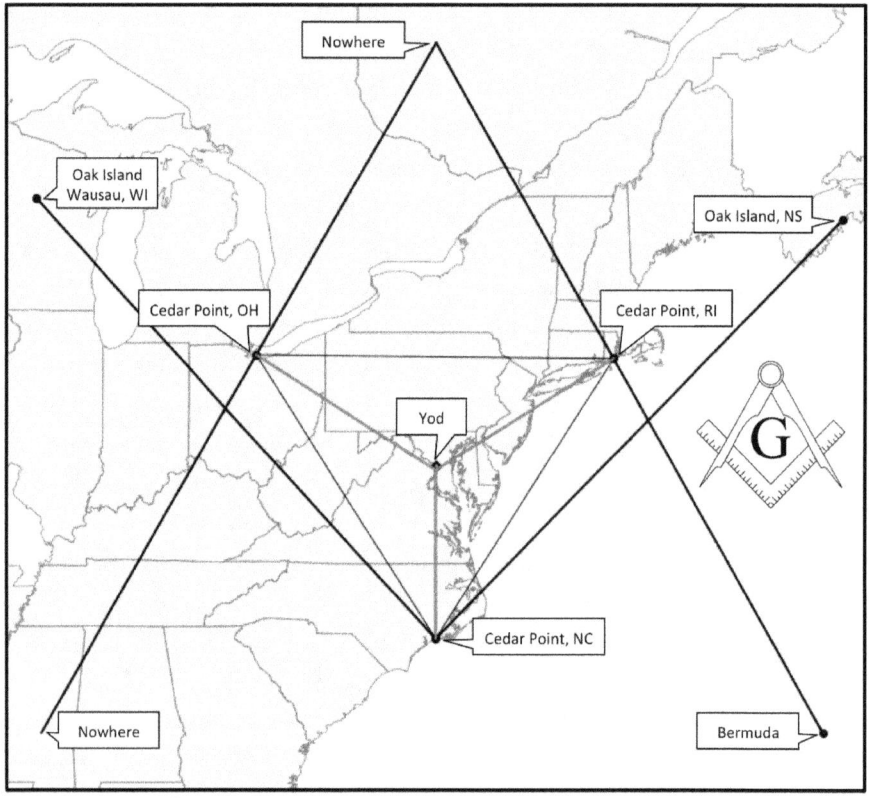

Figure 21: Possible Masonic Compass & Square with Yod (Yahweh) in center.

Fun With Numbers

The conspiracy theorists cry conspiracy because there *is* something unexplained going on. Well, ok, some of them are crazy, and some of them are stupid—let's be honest—but most of them are normal people who saw something odd that they could not explain. Ours is a big world with many things beyond our knowledge base. But, problematically, they tend to also lack the discipline and drive to explore the question marks thoroughly, factually, open-mindedly, yet logically, leaving open the most likely conclusion for them to draw—that there is insufficient evidence to form a conclusion. But there is something unexplained, which alone does not mean a conspiracy by secret rulers of the world. It is my observation that a primary source of illogic in this genre stems from a misunderstanding of numbers. And this book is filled with a lot of numbers.

Only the creators of this pattern know what the numbers meant to them, but I will catalog a few ideas with the intent to aid future researchers. Up front, though, I will make it clear to the reader that I consider these numeric games to have symbolic meanings to humans, but not real meanings in the universe. Many of the games that folks play with numbers, aiming to find some Truth about the universe, are tied to specific manmade mathematical constructs. Mathematics is an imperfect pairing of language and logic. Although the reader is likely to be only familiar with one mathematical construct, the one taught in grade school and used for most mathematical applications, other constructs exist; other systems of digits; other rule sets for addition, subtraction, multiplication, and division; etc. (e.g., lookup Abelian group) For example, the word amen "sums" to 33 (Freemasons!) if we use the *modern 26-letter English alphabet* and assign to each letter a numeric value, which is not a convention of the English language. A=1, M=13, E=5, N=14. 1+13+5+14=33. But that does not mean that the word amen is in any way equated with the number 33, as some on the Internet claim. This correlation is merely a modern coincidence in the English culture. Even number games played with the number nine (to show its special importance) immediately lose their way when we deviate from a manmade base-10 number system. In binary, the system that computers can process, the digit 9 does not exist— only zeros and ones. So the game wherein all multiples of 9 sum to 9 falls apart (e.g., 9x3 = 27 = 2+7 = 9, and so on). For example, in hexadecimal, 9x3 equals 1B, the digits of which sum to C (which is equivalent to the decimal number 12). If you don't know what that means, then my point is made. So, tread carefully on efforts to use numbers to find universal Truths. The universe may be symbolized by the Pythagorean Monad, the number 1, but the universe is not actually the number 1. Or is it?! No.

There is a practical purpose for choosing some of the numbers at play here. For example, why in the world would one choose to divide a circle into 360 degrees, rather than 100 degrees, or 400 degrees (the gradient)? Some might conclude that this decision pertains to the days of the year, noting that some ancient cultures used a 360-day year. Maybe. Add to that notion a more practical explanation. Just a few decades ago, before we all had portable computers and calculators, folks had to rely on hand calculations or mental calculations. Math can be hard, so one should do their utmost to make the common calculations as easy as possible. A number like 360 is a highly factorable number. It is easily divided by 2, 3, 4, 5, 6, 8, 9, 10, 12,... and so on. It is easy to calculate fractions of a full circle when we divide it into 360 degrees. There are 24 hours in a day. The number 24 equals 1x2x3x4, so it can be easily divided by 2, 3, 4, 6, 8, 12. This fact makes it easy to compute fractions of a day. Often the simplest answer is the correct one. The ancients that devised these systems probably did so for practical purposes, and then they devised a philosophy around that practical framework.

If Pike's work is to be trusted as authoritative, as its seems to me to be, then we can conclude from it that Freemasonry inherits much of its numeric symbolism from the Qabalah and from Pythagorean philosophy. I'll admit up front that I did not conduct a thorough research of this topic, as it tended to distract from the investigation that led to this book, but I had to familiarize myself with its basic concepts to translate some of Pike's denser passages. The key points, when it comes to understanding the symbolic meaning of numbers, come from the representation of the Infinite Deity—the one that we cannot ever glimpse—by the number 1, the Monad, and the production from that of all other things, revealed in layers through mathematical operations.[92] I'll break that down. There exists a single, yet infinite entity, unlike anything that we can comprehend, spoken of by Freemasons as Light or Reason, that *is* everything. Pike:

> "Before the chaos, that preceded the birth of Heaven and Earth," said the Chinese Lao-Tseu, "a single Being existed, immense and silent, immutable and always acting; the mother of the Universe. I know not the name of that Being, but I designate it by the word Reason. Man has his model in the earth, the earth in Heaven, Heaven in Reason, and Reason in itself."

This Infinite Deity is One. It cannot be divided in anyway. All that is and that will ever be will exist within this One. Since the Infinite Deity cannot be glimpsed himself he is only seen (not by us, but by higher beings) as a reflection of the One. With this reflection we have One plus one, which equals two. Two is a line, which only exists in one dimension. From One and two we can see the first number, which is three, the Trinity, represented by the triangle. From there, one can create other numbers through mathematical operations involving 1, 2, and 3. The triangle only exists in two dimensions. The square only exists in two dimensions. The first three-dimensional shape is the cube, which has six sides (1+2+3=6, and 1x2x3=6). If one puts a point in the center of the cube, giving a value of seven (six sides plus one center point), then the cube is formed of six pyramids, each pointing to the center of the cube. Take a moment to visualize that. You now have the gist of a geometric framework that starts with the One Infinite Deity, and through emanations, symbolized by mathematical operations, leads you to a concept of the material world, the three-dimensional cube, the four elements, the five senses, etc.

---

[92] http://en.wikipedia.org/wiki/Monad_(philosophy)

In math there are two operations that combine values: addition and multiplication. These two operations can be viewed symbolically as means of emanating from the One, through lesser Gods, Angels, whatever, until they eventually arrive at our bodies in the material world. Openly, Pike and others use addition to perform these sorts of number games. I'll cover some of them in a moment. But, I think that a combination of multiplication with addition is a secret part of Freemasonry's numeric symbolism. I'm way out on a limb here, but there are some odd correlations that should not be discounted outright. And remember: being open-minded does not mean believing.

33. I speculate that in Freemasonry there are three gods at some level beneath the infinite Deity. The infinite Deity is represented by the Monad (1) and the other three are each represented by the number 33. This is just a guess. Here is my derivation of this point.

The works of Pythagoras, which have been lost to time, are speculated to include a derivation of the number 10 as *a* "perfect" number. This derivation stems from the Hebrew name of the Deity, which was formed by four characters. In English these characters are YHWH: Yahweh, or Jehovah. In Hebrew they are written right-to-left: HWHY. These letters can be expressed triangularly.[93]

H

H W

H W H

H W H Y

Count the number of letters in each row to get the numbers 1, 2, 3, and 4. They can be added to form any decimal digit. For example, 5 = 1+4; 7 = 3+4; but most importantly, 1+2+3+4 = 10. This last combination is the reason that 10 is considered a perfect number. In Pythagorean (and Qabalah) philosophy these letters are the Word of God, the creative force that came from the Infinite Deity. But, 10 is not the most perfect number (I theorize). We have only used the mathematical operation of addition (1+2+3+4 = 10). What about multiplication? Well, 1x2x3x4 = 24. Does this make 24 more perfect than 10? If 10 is the Word of God, what does 24 symbolize? I don't know. I think it's a secret. But, Hall offers a possible clue:

---

[93] Pike, Albert. (1871) *Morals and Dogma.*

The cube also consists of six pyramids with the six surfaces of the cube as their bases. The points of these six pyramids meet at the center of the cube. **These six pyramids, each consisting of four triangles, signify the elements, and produce the magical number 24 [6x4], which refers to the Elders before the Throne.** The six surfaces and the point constitute the magical number 7. If 7 be multiplied by 7 again, and so on 7 times, the answer will reveal the method used by the ancients for measuring the periods of eternity; thus: (1) 7 X 7 = 49; (2) 49 X 7 = 343; (3) 343 X 7 = 2,401; (4) 2,401 X 7 =16,807; (5):16,807 X 7 = 117,649; (6) 117,649 X 7 = 823,543; (7) 823,543 X 7 = 5,764,801. (This is not to be taken as earth years or times.) The 5,000,000 represents the great hall year; the 700,000 the great Sabbath year, wherein all human beings gradually gain true understanding and become heirs to their original and eternal inheritance, which was lost when they were enmeshed in the lower elements. The 64,800 is the number of the fallen angels, and the last one year signifies the liberation of Lucifer and return to his original estate.

I had to lookup the Elders before the Throne. They are mentioned in The Book of Revelation: "Surrounding the throne were twenty-four other thrones, and seated on them were twenty-four elders. They were dressed in white and had crowns of gold on their heads." Purity (white) and light (gold). Back to our math homework, what if we combine addition and multiplication to get an even more perfect number?

The factorial is a mathematical function that multiplies an integer by all integers smaller than itself (down to 1). So, 4-factorial, written 4!, is 4x3x2x1 = 24. Similarly, 3! = 6, 2! = 2, and 1! = 1. Ten is the sum of all integers from 1 to 4, whereas 24 is the product (multiplication) of all integers from 1 to 4. Is 10 (the sum) more perfect than 24 (the product)? What if we combine the two operations? What does 4!+3!+2!+1! equal? It equals 24+6+2+1 = 33. Thirty-three is the most-perfect number because it is a combination of addition and multiplication of digits related to the name of the Deity.

If we take three (a Trinity) of the number 33, then we get 99 (the direction faced by the front door of the GW MM). Add the Monad (1) and we get 99+1 = 100, or 10 squared. Washington DC is a 10x10 mile square. This *feels* right, right?

There are 33 vertebrae in the spine, so some suggest that 33 represents these vertebrae, as one ascends from their basest form up the 33 degrees of

Scottish Rite Masonry to the Reasoning part of them (usually found in the brain). That's a nice story, but I strongly suspect that Masonry's reason for having 33 degrees involves more than the vertebrae, as there are strong Pythagorean mathematical philosophical threads throughout its construct, and Freemasonry is openly described as a Geometry.

720. My favorite number in the Tree of Life template (Figure 2) is 720. Obviously, it equals 2x360, as in 360 degrees in a complete circle. This meaning is relevant to this investigation, since angles are the predominant building block.

720 equals 6! (six factorial). 6! = 1x2x3x4x5x6. The factorial comes up a few times in our numbers. Five factorial is 120 (1x2x3x4x5), which is the angle between our sunrise, midday, and sunset azimuths at the GW MM. The Tree of Life length is 1152 feet, which is 2x576. 576 equals 24 squared (24x24). There are 24 hours in a day. If you create a right triangle with one angle equal to 66 degrees, then the other angle is 24 (90 = 66+24). 24 is 4 factorial (1x2x3x4). Now, back to 720. 720=3x240. Anything multiplied by three might symbolize a Trinity. So, what is the importance of 240? The number 10 was considered a perfect number by Pythagoras and by the makers of the Qabalah (the Tree of Life is made of 10 Sephiroth, 10 emanations breathed by the Word of God). Anyway, 10 = 1+2+3+4 and 24 = 1x2x3x4.

240 = 10x24. So,

240 = (1+2+3+4)x(1x2x3x4) = 2x(1x2x3x4x5)

720 = 3x(1+2+3+4)x(1x2x3x4) = (1x2x3x4x5x6)

I think that's pretty cool. It *feels* right, right?

The sum of all numbers from 1 to some number also comes up a few times in this investigation. I just showed that 10 is the sum of all integers from 1 to 4. 66, our other favorite number, is the sum of all integers from 1 to 11 (66 = 1+2+3+...+11). How many times have we seen 11? It divides 22 (the number of paths on the Tree of Life; Lodge 22 is at the GW MM), 33, 66, 99. 120 is the sum of all integers from 1 to 15 (Lodge 120 is at the GW MM). 15 is the sum of all integers from 1 to 5. Everyone's least favorite number, 666, equals the sum of all integers from 1 to 36 (6 squared).[94] Lucifer's number, 741, is the sum of all integers from 1 to 38.

---

[94] If 666 is your favorite number then you're trying too hard to be edgy.

I'll end this appendix as all appendices should end, with an Amen. I hope that you agree that the word amen does not "sum" to 33, even though its modern English letters can be added this way. The word amen has been around much longer than the English language. If amen is written in its original Hebrew (AMN), a language in which all letters correspond with a number (unlike English), then it has an interesting numerical value. A=1, M=40, N(final)=700. 1+40+700=741, the number for Lucifer.

There *is* something unexplained going on. Amen.

Geo-Coordinates

Here is a list of geo-coordinates used during this investigation. The list is not complete, but it is enough to verify my calculations and further them if desired.

Oak Island
Tree of Life coordinates, as reported by Petter Amundsen.
(44.51518578,-64.29224436) Point [3]
(44.51373661,-64.29295547) Point [6]
(44.51333381,-64.29392383) Point [9]
(44.51294067,-64.29486483) Point [10]

Rhode Island
(41.485818, -71.309856) Newport Tower
(41.486375, -71.308255) George Washington statue, Redwood Library
(41.404704, -71.493410) Cedar Point peninsula

Long Island
(41.028022, -72.225605) Cedar Point Rd, Cedar Point County Park

Manhattan, New York City

(40.779612, -73.965419) Cleopatra's Needle
(40.742738, -73.988985) Worth Monument
(40.711083, -74.009167) Emmet obelisk, St. Paul's Chapel
(40.708414, -74.011469) Soldier's Monument spire, Trinity Church cemetery
(40.753250, -73.982361) New York Public Library, main branch
(40.748392, -73.985618) Empire State Building
(40.705317, -74.012941) 26 Broadway, beneath pyramid
(40.761622, -73.970146) Ritz Plaza
(40.730539, -73.996823) Garibaldi statue, Washington Square
(40.769823, -73.972353) Shakespeare statue, Central Park
(40.769903, -73.972777) Columbus statue, Central Park
(40.689258, -74.044567) Statue of Liberty
(40.690580, -74.045682) Liberty Island flag pole
(40.688591, -74.043985) Point [10] of Liberty Island TOL

Alexandria, Virginia

(38.804118, -77.039402) Kings St, at waterfront (Y in sidewalk)
(38.806753, -77.062434) Alexandria War Dead Monument
(38.807499, -77.065917) George Washington Masonic National Memorial,
                         beneath tower
(38.807055, -77.062436) Point [10] of GW MM TOL

Washington, District of Columbia

(38.897637, -77.036534) White House
(38.900273, -77.036547) Point [10] of White House TOL
(38.889800, -77.009199) U.S. Capital Building, beneath the dome
(38.913549, -77.036507) Scottish Rite HQ (House of the Temple), center of
                         16th St in front of Temple
(38.870945, -77.055966) Pentagon, center
(38.881400, -77.036522) Jefferson Memorial
(38.889483, -77.035223) Washington Monument

Sandusky (Cedar Point), Ohio

(41.453022, -82.712577) Point [10] of Sandusky TOL
(41.455178, -82.709393) Masonic Compass and Square display
(41.485818, -82.682355) Cedar Point, due west of Newport Tower

North Carolina

(34.686414, -77.086454) Octagon House, on Masonic Campus in
                          Cedar Point, NC
(35.171947, -80.797307) Scottish Rite Temple, Charlotte, NC
(34.683262, -77.062436) Cedar Point, NC. Point chosen at intersection of
line bearing due south from GW MM TOL point [10], and line from Scottish
Rite Temple (Charlotte) through Octagon House (which bears 279.0/99.0
degrees, similar to GW MM TOL).

Wisconsin

(44.950005, -89.628085) Oak Island, Wausau, Wisconsin

Bermuda

(32.280800, -64.886524) Western side of islands

Geodesic Analysis

I encourage the reader to reproduce my analysis, uncover any errors that I may have made, improve upon my processes, and discover new elements of this secret plan. I sense that I have only touched the surface of this mystery. This appendix provides the reader with the details of my analysis and the code used to discover geographic alignments. I consider this to be one of the primary strengths of this analysis, that it is quantifiable and reproducible, rather than the circumstantial and subjective analyses that dominate this field. The technical work was performed using Mathematica version 10, which is available for home use. As explained in the book, Google Earth does not possess the ability to calculate rhumb lines, so I needed a program that could. Mathematica was a nice fit. If you do not have Mathematica, then this appendix will not be of much value to you.

Disclaimer: What follows is a brief introduction to Mathematica, with an emphasis on its geographics functions. The reader applies this information at the reader's own risk. In other words, if my code does not work as you expected it to, then you are on your own to figure it out. I am in no way liable for whatever harm you might endure as a result of this, or any other, chapter in this book.

An Introduction to Geodesic Analysis Using Mathematica v10

This appendix introduces the reader to Mathematica v10 and the geographic tools that I used during my analysis. This introduction is by no means a thorough course on Mathematica, geodesic analysis, or the geographic tools available in Mathematica. Rather, I aim to arm you with the tools needed to understand my analytic process, evaluate the accuracy and completeness of my work, and further it if desired. Open a new Mathematica "notebook" and follow along. After entering each group of commands, press shift-enter to execute them.

Before we dive into Mathematica's geographic toolkit, I will cover four programming basics needed to understand my use of the geographic tools: variables (and assignment, generally), lists, functions, and multi-statement code.

In any programming language one needs the ability to assign values, functions, and other things to convenient names. For example, if one were performing a large number of mathematical calculations in their program they might want to create a variable called pi so their equation for the circumference of a circle looks like this (`C = 2*pi*r`) and not like this (`C = 2*3.141592654*r`). In this case, I used the equal sign (=) to define my formula. In mathematica, the equal sign (=) performs what is called an "immediate assignment," meaning that it places the value on the right into memory under the name on the left as soon as this line in the code is encountered by Mathematica. For constants, such as pi, an immediate assignment makes sense. But, it does not work in some cases. For example, consider this expression:

```
randomnumber = Random[100]
```

The function on the right comes with Mathematica (I did not need to write it), and it will return a random integer between 1 and 100. When this line is encountered `Random[100]` will return a number and that number will be assigned to the name `randomnumber`. Let's pretend that it returned the number 33. Every time that the user calls `randomnumber` it will give them a value of 33. It was random once, at the time of the original call, and never again. If we use colon-equal (:=) rather than equal (=) then, in

Mathematica, we will be performing a "delayed assignment." So, let's write our line this way:

```
randomnumber := Random[100]
```

The delayed assignment means that the right side of the equation is executed every time that randomnumber is called, and not merely the first time. So, each time we call randomnumber we get a different randomnumber. A delayed assignment has another benefit that may be important if your programs get large. One can assign more complex structures to a variable name than merely a single number. If the coder uses an immediate assignment then the right side of the equation is placed in memory and held there, even if not used, which in large programs can create memory problems (as unneeded variables take up RAM space), and the power drain that results. In my code, you will see both of these assignments used for reasons that made sense to me.

Imagine that you have several related values that you want to place under the same name. To do this, you will use a list (also called an array). We will encounter lists often in geographic analysis. In Mathematica a list is represented by curly-braces

```
list1 = {147,66,360,213}
```

In Mathematica, the first value in the list is assigned index one, whereas other computer languages tend to reference this first spot by the index zero. So, the first index of list1 is 147. We access it using double brackets: list1[[1]].

Our next programming basic involves the creation of a function. Mathematica provides a flexible underlying framework that underpins the code that I am about to show you. It is worth deeper investigation by an interested reader. But for our purposes, I will cover only the surface level. Let's return to our equation for the circumference of a circle. If I want to turn that equation into a function that I can call anytime, the I will use code like this:

```
circumference[radius_] := 2*Pi*radius
```

I will execute the function for a radius of 2 by calling it this way: circumference[2]. The underline following the variable "radius" tells

Mathematica that radius is a variable (or, more specifically, a "pattern") which can be used to represent just about anything. If I call `circumference["Bob"]` then Mathematica will return (`2 Pi Bob`), where `Pi` is the Greek letter and not the English letters shown here. We can limit the type of pattern that Mathematica will accept for radius by including pattern type after the underline, e.g., `circumference[radius_Integer] := 2*Pi*radius` will only accept integer values for radius. For this function, the variable named radius is only valid within the definition of the function and not in other parts of the program. In other words, its memory assignment is "local" to the function `circumference`.

Our final programming basic (in Mathematica) involves the use of multi-statement code. I'll use the circumference equation as an example. Ignoring the fact that Mathematica has a built-in variable called `Pi`, I will create one called pi (lower case) so that I do not need to type out the digits in my formula. I will then calculate the circumference. To put these two distinct operations (assigning a value to a variable and executing an equation) in the same execution statement, I separate them by a semi-colon.

```
pi=3.141592654; radius=2; 2*pi*radius
```

By using this approach, creating the variables pi and radius as separate but adjoined statements, I am creating variables pi and radius that will live beyond the execution of the line. In other words, variables will remain in memory that assigned the names pi and radius to the digits shown. They are "global" variables. Later, I will reveal a Mathematica programming tool that allows the creation of a temporary variable that is only available to the function that created it.

Let's move on to geographic tools. Every point on the Earth can be represented by a geographic coordinate (geocoord). We will use angular units for our geocoords, namely latitude and longitude. Consider a point at the center of the Earth. It is the center of the three-dimensional ellipse that we use to mathematically represent the Earth. If you draw a line from this point to the equator (anywhere on the equator) then that line points at zero degrees latitude. If that line pointed at the north pole, then it would be at 90 degrees latitude. If it pointed at the south pole, then it would be at -90 degrees latitude. Positive latitude values point to the northern hemisphere. There exists a shortest-path (geodesic) line that is drawn from the south pole to the north pole and passes through a specific point in England. It is called the Prime Meridian. Any line from the center of the Earth to this meridian has a longitude of zero degrees. Any line to the west of this meridian has negative values for longitude. Any line to the east has positive values for longitude. The point on the surface of the Earth at the end of our imaginary line is a geographic coordinate. Since we are only considering geographic coordinates in North America, all of our geocoords have positive values of latitude and negative values of longitude.

In Mathematica, one creates a geocoord that Mathematica can understand using the GeoPosition function.

```
GeoPosition[{latitude_in_degrees,
             longitude_in_degrees,
             elevation_in_meters},
            datum]
```

The elevation field is optional. I have not found it particularly useful in this work, given how Mathematica treats it. So, I leave it blank. Datum is the reference ellipsoid, the name of the mathematical model that approximates the shape of Earth. For this investigation I used "ITRF00", which stands for International Terrestrial Reference Frame (2000). There are several ways to represent latitude and longitude values. I'll give an example of two of them here: decimal and Degrees-Minutes-Seconds (DMS). Here is Point [10] of the Oak Island Tree of Life using decimal and DMS notation. Note that when using DMS, one must use a function that understands it (FromDMS). Also note that I place the negative sign (indicating West) in front of the FromDMS function and not inside, e.g., -64. Placing the negative sign inside FromDMS would give in an erroneous result because of the means by which the function processes its inputs.

```
GeoPosition[{44.51294067,-64.29486483},"ITRF00"]
GeoPosition[{
    FromDMS[{44,30,46.5864}],
    -FromDMS[{64,17,41.5134}]},
    "ITRF00"]
```

In this work I have exclusively used rhumb lines, rather than geodesic lines. In Mathematica, this parameter is set by what is called the pathtype. Several of Mathematica's geographic functions do not allow for the specification of pathtype; they inherently use a geodesic path. This unchangeable parameter renders these functions useless to me. So, if I want to determine the distance between two geographic coordinates (point1, point2), then Mathematica's built-in function `GeoDistance[point1,point2]` is unhelpful. If I want to determine the azimuth between these two points, then `GeoDirection[point1,point2]` is useless to me. They assume that the user wants `pathtype = "Geodesic"`. Instead, I must use the Mathematica function that allows me to specify pathtype. It can take two types of inputs.

```
GeoDisplacement[point1,point2,pathtype]
GeoDisplacement[{distance_in_meters,azimuth},pathtype]
```

`GeoDisplacement` returns its output as a list `{{distance_in_meters,azimuth},pathtype}`. The first element in the list is also a list `{distance_in_meters,azimuth}`. The first element in that second list is a distance (in meters), and the second value is an azimuth (in angular degrees). Here's an example, which assumes that point1 and point2 are variables of type `GeoPosition`:

```
distanceandbearing = GeoDisplacement[point1,point2,pathtype];
distanceandbearing[[1]][[1]] (* distance between points *)
distanceandbearing[[1]][[2]] (* azimuth between points *)
```

I created my own version of `GeoDistance` and `GeoDirection` using `GeoDisplacement`, which allowed me to specify the pathtype. Note that Mathematica is "case sensitive," meaning that a capital letter is read as different than a lower-case letter. So, these variables are different: var, Var. As such, I can use the name `geodistance` because it is different than `GeoDistance`, which is already taken by Mathematica.

```
geodistance[point1_,point2_,pathtype_] :=
    GeoDisplacement[point1,point2,pathtype][[1]][[1]]

geoazimuth[point1_,point2_,pathtype_] :=
    GeoDisplacement[point1,point2,pathtype][[1]][[2]]
```

Using these new functions makes my code more readable than if I used `GeoDisplacement` and the list indices. Let's calculate the distance between the Pentagon and the U.S. Capital building, and divide that distance by the length of the Oak Island Tree of Life (1152 feet).

```
ftpm = 3.280839895;   (* feet per meter *)
uscapital = GeoPosition[{38.889800,-77.009199},"ITRF00"];
pentagon = GeoPosition[{38.870945,-77.055966},"ITRF00"];
geodistance[pentagon,uscapital,"Rhumb"]*ftpm/1152
```

Result: 13.00401669

What if we know our starting point and we want to determine the geocoordinate at a certain distance along a certain path, e.g., 300 miles due north of the White House? How do we do that? Mathematica has a function called `GeoDestination` that performs this task, but it can be easily misused. For example, one could do this:

```
GeoDestination[point1,distance_in_meters,azimuth]
```

This approach will return the destination along a geodesic path. We do not use geodesic paths in this analysis. So, we would use instead:

```
GeoDestination[
    point1,
    GeoDisplacement[
        {distance_in_meters,azimuth},
        pathtype]
    ]
```

That is a bit bulky, so I created my own `geodestination` function.

```
geodestination[point_,distance_,azimuth_,pathtype_] :=
    GeoDestination[
        point,
        GeoDisplacement[{distance,azimuth},pathtype]]
```

Now, I can perform this calculation by simply calling my own function (the left side of the equation) without needing to type out the right side of the equation each time.

What if we have two points and we want to use them to define a line that extends beyond them? For that case, I created a function that extends a line between two points beyond the second point.

```
geoextensionpt[point1_,point2_,scale_,pathtype_] :=
    geodestination[point1,
        scale*geodistance[point1,point2,pathtype],
        geoazimuth[point1,point2,pathtype],
        pathtype]
```

The "scale" parameter allows me to extend the line to a distance that is a multiple of the distance between the two points. So, calling `geoextensionpt[p1,p2,2,"Rhumb"]` returns a geocoordinate that is twice as far from p1 as p2 is from p1. I end my function name with the letters "pt" to specify that this function returns a single point (`GeoPosition`); read its name as Geo-Extension-Point. In a moment I will create a similar function that returns a "path" through these points.

We are almost ready to begin creating maps using Mathematica. Before we do we must add one more element to our toolkit, the geographic path: `GeoPath`. Mathematica will interpret paths as lines when it draws graphical elements. `GeoPath` has several forms.

```
(* path between two points *)
GeoPath[{point1,point2},pathtype]
(* closed path *)
GeoPath[{point1,point2,point3,point1},pathtype]
(* path from point1 for given distance *)
GeoPath[{point1,distance_in_meters,azimuth},pathtype]
```

Here is my function that extends a path from one point through a second point.

```
geoextensionpath[point1_,point2_,scale_,pathtype_] :=
    GeoPath[{
        point1,
        geoextensionpt[point1,point2,scale,pathtype]},
        pathtype]
```

Now that we have covered our Mathematica basics, let's draw our first map. We will create a Mercator projection that shows a point at the White

House, U.S. Capital Building, and Pentagon, and draws a path (line) between these three points. To do this, we use the GeoGraphics function, which requires a list of geographic elements, such as points and paths, and can be tailored by setting various parameters. Mathematica must have access to the Internet to perform geographic calculations since some of its data is pulled from Wolfram|Alpha servers.

```
datum = "ITRF00";
uscapital = GeoPosition[{38.889800, -77.009199}, datum];
whitehouse = GeoPosition[{38.897637, -77.036534}, datum];
pentagon = GeoPosition[{38.870945, -77.055966}, datum];
GeoGraphics[ {
    Point[ { whitehouse,uscapital,pentagon } ],
    GeoPath[ { whitehouse,uscapital,pentagon },"Rhumb"]
  },
  GeoProjection->"Mercator"]
```

Press shift-enter after typing this code into your Mathematica notebook to create the map. GeoProjection is an option for the function GeoGraphics. The value of an option is set using the arrow, as shown above. Let's change the color and style of the line, increase the point size, center the map over the White House, and specify the size (range, in meters) of our map.

```
GeoGraphics[ {
    PointSize[0.005], (* fraction of map size *)
    Point[ { whitehouse,uscapital,pentagon } ],
    Red,Dashed,
    GeoPath[ { whitehouse,uscapital,pentagon },"Rhumb"]
  },
  GeoProjection->"Mercator",
  GeoCenter->whitehouse,
  GeoRange->6000
]
```

I leave it to the studious reader to develop a full understanding of these commands using Mathematica's built-in help library. I want to offer here a few more useful functions. But first, I must introduce the reader to a Mathematica Module, which is equivalent to a procedure or function in most programming languages. It allows the user to create local variables and group multiple commands under a single name. Its basic form is:

```
Module[{local1,local2=default2,etc.},
       commands]
```

Below are two functions of my own design, lineintersection and midpoint. lineintersection is used to find a GeoPosition (point) at the intersection of two lines, each defined by its two end points. The function will return incorrect results if the two lines do not actually cross. midpoint returns a GeoPosition at the center of a line defined by two points. These functions allow the user to specify the path type, such as "Rhumb" or "Geodesic". Note the use of my own functions, such as geoazimuth, defined earlier. Note the usage element at the bottom, which is a feature of Mathematica. If I type ? lineintersection <shift-enter> into a notebook containing this function, then a help dialogue will be shown. In the functions, I create a few local variables (e.g., p1) that are merely shorter representations of their originals (e.g., point1), which makes the code readable, yet more condensed internally. I use indentation here to aid the reader, but it is not necessary to Mathematica.

```
midpoint[point1_,point2_,pathtype_] :=
  Module[{p1=point1,p2=point2,pt=pathtype,dist,az},
    az = GeoDisplacement[p1,p2,pt][[1]][[2]];
    dist = GeoDisplacement[p1,p2,pt][[1]][[1]]/2;
    Return[GeoDestination[p1,GeoDisplacement[{dist,az},pt]]]]]

lineintersection[path1pt1_,path1pt2_,
                 path2pt1_,path2pt2_,
                 pathtype_] := Module[
    {p11=path1pt1,p12=path1pt2,
     p21=path2pt1,p22=path2pt2,
     az211,az212,az1,az2,d,tolerance,
     m,azm,maxcount,count},
    maxcount = 300;
    tolerance = 1;
    d = tolerance + 1;
    az211 = geoazimuth[p21,p11,pathtype];
    az212 = geoazimuth[p21,p12,pathtype];
    (* Normalize *)
    If[(Abs[az211] > 90 && Abs[az212] > 90),
       {p21, p22} = {p22, p21}; (* swap *)
       az211 = geoazimuth[p21, p11, pathtype];
       az212 = geoazimuth[p21, p12, pathtype]];
    az2 = geoazimuth[p21, p22, pathtype];
    (* Convert to case 1 : p11 CW of p21 *)
```

```
If[(az211 >= az2) && (az2 >= az212),
    {p11, p12} = {p12, p11}];
az1 = geoazimuth[p11, p12, pathtype];
count = 0;
While[d > tolerance && count < maxcount,
  m = geodestination[p11,
          geodistance[p11,p12,pathtype]/2.0,
          az1,pathtype];
  azm = geoazimuth[p21, m, pathtype];
  If[(azm > az2),p12=m,p11=m];
  d = geodistance[p11, p12, pathtype];
  count++
]; (* end While *)
Return[geodestination[p11,
          geodistance[p11,p12,pathtype]/2.0,
          az1,
          pathtype]]
]
lineintersection::usage = "lineintersection[path1_pt1,
path1_pt2, path2_pt1, path2_pt2, pathtype] - returns
GeoPosition at intersection of two paths, each defined by two
points.";
```

The following code defines a function that can be used to find the azimuth of the sun at sunset and sunrise on the solstices and equinoxes. The season and event (rise or set) must have the first letter capitalized and be enclosed in quotes (match what's in the code). I include an example below.

```
solsticeaz[loc_,season_,event_] := Module[
    {time,sumsoldate,winsoldate,sprsoldate,autsoldate,
    ftpm,mpmi},
    sumsoldate = DateObject[{2014,6,21,0,0}];
    winsoldate = DateObject[{2014,12,21,0,0}];
    sprsoldate = DateObject[{2014,3,20,0,0}];
    autsoldate = DateObject[{2014,9,23,0,0}];
    ftpm = 3.280839895;  (* feet per meter *)
    mpmi = 5280/ftpm;    (*meters per mile*)
    time = "Error";
    time = Which[
    season == "Autumn" && event == "Rise",
        Sunrise[{Latitude[loc], Longitude[loc]},autsoldate],
        season == "Autumn" && event == "Set",
        Sunset[{Latitude[loc], Longitude[loc]},autsoldate],
        season == "Spring" && event == "Rise",
        Sunrise[{Latitude[loc], Longitude[loc]},sprsoldate],
```

```
      season == "Spring" && event == "Set",
      Sunset[{Latitude[loc], Longitude[loc]},sprsoldate],
      season == "Summer" && event == "Rise",
      Sunrise[{Latitude[loc], Longitude[loc]},sumsoldate],
      season == "Summer" && event == "Set",
      Sunset[{Latitude[loc], Longitude[loc]},sumsoldate],
      season == "Winter" && event == "Rise",
      Sunrise[{Latitude[loc], Longitude[loc]},winsoldate],
      season == "Winter" && event == "Set",
      Sunset[{Latitude[loc], Longitude[loc]},winsoldate]
   ];
   FromDMS[StarData["Sun",EntityProperty["Star",
      "Azimuth",{"Date"->time,"Location"->loc}]]]]
solsticeaz::usage =
  "solsticeaz[loc,season,event], where season =
Winter,Summer,Autumn,Spring; event = Rise, Set";
```

Let's use `solsticeaz` to calculate the summer solstice sunset azimuths at the Statue of Liberty and the George Washington Masonic National Memorial. Enter these lines of code in a Mathematica notebook, then press shift-enter.

```
statueofliberty = GeoPosition[{40.689258,-74.044567},
   "ITRF00"];
gwmasonicmemorial = GeoPosition[{38.80749855,-77.06591674},
   "ITRF00"];
solsticeaz[statueofliberty, "Summer", "Set"]
solsticeaz[gwmasonicmemorial, "Summer", "Set"]
```

The results are 302.406 (for the SOL) and 301.403 (for the GW MM). They differ by a few thousandths of a degree. When I first ran this, about nine months before I wrote these words, the results only differed by one one-thousandth of a degree (so Mathematica has changed its data a bit). I find it interesting that these azimuths differ by exactly one degree.

The following code defines a function that can be used to create a GeoPath of a given distance (in miles) from a GeoPosition, along a solstice or equinox sunrise or sunset azimuth, using a given pathtype. I include an example below.

```
solsticepath[loc_,dist_,season_,event_,pathtype_] := Module[
   {time,az,sumsoldate,winsoldate,sprsoldate,
   autsoldate,ftpm,mpmi},
```

```
sumsoldate = DateObject[{2014,6,21,0,0}];
winsoldate = DateObject[{2014,12,21,0,0}];
sprsoldate = DateObject[{2014,3,20,0,0}];
autsoldate = DateObject[{2014,9,23,0,0}];
ftpm = 3.280839895;   (* feet per meter *)
mpmi = 5280/ftpm;     (*meters per mile*)
time = "Error";
time = Which[
    season == "Autumn" && event == "Rise",
    Sunrise[{Latitude[loc],Longitude[loc]},autsoldate],
    season == "Autumn" && event == "Set",
    Sunset[{Latitude[loc],Longitude[loc]},autsoldate],
    season == "Spring" && event == "Rise",
    Sunrise[{Latitude[loc],Longitude[loc]},sprsoldate],
    season == "Spring" && event == "Set",
    Sunset[{Latitude[loc],Longitude[loc]},sprsoldate],
    season == "Summer" && event == "Rise",
    Sunrise[{Latitude[loc],Longitude[loc]},sumsoldate],
    season == "Summer" && event == "Set",
    Sunset[{Latitude[loc],Longitude[loc]},sumsoldate],
    season == "Winter" && event == "Rise",
    Sunrise[{Latitude[loc],Longitude[loc]},winsoldate],
    season == "Winter" && event == "Set",
    Sunset[{Latitude[loc],Longitude[loc]},winsoldate]
];
az = FromDMS[StarData["Sun",EntityProperty["Star",
    "Azimuth",{"Date"->time,"Location"->loc}]]];
Print[az, "  ",
    geodestination[loc,dist*mpmi,az,pathtype]];
GeoPath[{loc,dist*mpmi,az},pathtype]
]
solsticepath::usage =
    "solsticepath[loc,dist_miles,season,event,pathtype]";
```

The following example creates a GeoPath from the Newport Tower at sunset on the winter solstice of a distance sufficient to reach the GW MM. If one were to plot this GeoPath using GeoGraphics, and zoom into the GW MM landscape using the GeoCenter and GeoRange parameters, then they would see that this path crosses the center of the landscape, as depicted in Figure 7.

```
nptower = GeoPosition[{41.485818, -71.309856}, "ITRF00"];
path = solsticepath[nptower, 400, "Winter", "Set", "Rhumb"];
<Add code here to plot this path using GeoGraphics>
```

Tree of Life Template. There are several ways by which a Tree of Life template can be made, depending on which points are the anchors, the pathtype, how each point is calculated, etc. I introduce here two functions: one that returns a list of points, and one that returns a list of paths between those points. The reader is encouraged to be very careful in using these templates, particularly for enlarged versions of the Tree of Life. Namely, the distortions on a Mercator projection are not always intuitively understood. For example, when Mathematica calculates a distance along a rhumb line, it calculates the *actual* distance along that line. If one were to take a printed version of a Mercator projection and use a ruler to draw their lines, then these hand-drawn lines would likely differ from the Mathematica-calculated lines, with lines further from the equator having greater distortions. None of this will matter when verifying my work until one attempts to reproduce the large TOL in the Epilogue. I created that graphic *before* I fully understood the Mercator projection and Mathematica's treatment of it. So here's a hint: the Epilogue is the Epilogue for a reason, deliberately *outside* the main body of the book. Note that the header of its pages does not claim to be part of "Deciphering the Map," but is part of "The Seal of Liberty." The body of the book exposes and solves a mystery. The Epilogue (and some appendices) creates a new, but related, mystery that the reader is encouraged to ponder. I placed clues throughout the book regarding the purpose of the Epilogue and the solution to its mystery. The Epilogue is factual and accurate as presented. I am not deceiving the reader, but I doubt that the reader grasped its meaning during their first read.

The following code creates a list of points in a Tree of Life pattern that can be used to test various locations for Tree of Life dimensions. It is anchored by a `GeoPosition` at point [10], and oriented by the azimuth from point [10] to point [1]. If scale is set to 1, then it will be 1152 feet long, otherwise it is 1152*scale feet long. In the comments, "BS" denotes the Buried Stone, and "KP" the Knowledge Point. A few other points are included that are not numbered on the TOL Template in Figure 2. An example at the GW MM is provided below.

```
TOLpoints[anchor_,θ_,scale_,pathtype_] := Module[
  {width,orient,zeroAZ,ninteyAZ,ninteynegAZ,GDisp,
   GDispninety,GDninetyneg},
  width = 360;
  orient[az_] := If[
```

```
    QuantityUnit[az]=="AngularDegrees",
    az,
    Quantity[az,"Degrees"]];
zeroAZ[az_] := orient[az];
ninetyAZ[az_] := orient[az]+Quantity[90,"Degrees"];
ninetynegAZ[az_] := orient[az]+Quantity[-90,"Degrees"];
GDisp[dist_,az_] :=
    GeoDisplacement[{scale*dist/ftpm,zeroAZ[az]},pathtype];
GDispninety[dist_, az_] :=
    GeoDisplacement[{scale*dist/ftpm,ninetyAZ[az]},pathtype];
GDispninetyneg[dist_, az_] :=
    GeoDisplacement[{scale*dist/ftpm,ninetynegAZ[az]},
        pathtype];
Return[{
    (* 1 *) GeoDestination[anchor,GDisp[1152,θ]],
    (* 2 *) GeoDestination[GeoDestination[
                anchor,GDisp[1005,θ]],GDispninety[width,θ]],
    (* 3 *) GeoDestination[GeoDestination[
                anchor,GDisp[1005,θ]],GDispninetyneg[width,θ]],
    (* 4 *) GeoDestination[GeoDestination[
                anchor,GDisp[723,θ]],GDispninety[width,θ]],
    (* 5 *) GeoDestination[GeoDestination[
                anchor,GDisp[723,θ]],GDispninetyneg[width,θ]],
    (* 6 *) GeoDestination[anchor,GDisp[576,θ]],
    (* 7 *) GeoDestination[GeoDestination[
                anchor,GDisp[429,θ]],GDispninety[width,θ]],
    (* 8 *) GeoDestination[GeoDestination[
                anchor,GDisp[429,θ]],GDispninetyneg[width,θ]],
    (* 9 *) GeoDestination[anchor,GDisp[282,θ]],
    (* 10 *) anchor,
    (* 11 *) GeoDestination[anchor,GDisp[1005,θ]], (* BS *)
    (* 12 *) GeoDestination[anchor,GDisp[141,θ]],
    (* 13 *) GeoDestination[anchor,GDisp[429,θ]],
    (* 14 *) GeoDestination[anchor,GDisp[864,θ]],   (* KP *)
    (* 15 *) GeoDestination[anchor,GDisp[936,θ]]
    }]
]
```

Using the template above, here is the code to generate the Tree of Life at the GW MM.

```
gwmm10 = GeoPosition[{38.807055, -77.062436}, "ITRF00"];
gwmmTOLpt := TOLpoints[gwmm10, 279.25, 1, "Rhumb"]
```

If you want the GeoPosition of, say, point [6], use:

```
gwmmTOLpt[[6]]
```

You can plot these points using GeoGraphics and the Point object, as such:

```
GeoGraphics[{Point[gwmmTOLpt]}, GeoProjection->"Mercator"]
```

The following code creates a list of GeoPath objects that can be used in GeoGraphics to display the Tree of Life paths. I included comments in the code to reveal its different parts, per my Masonic Tree of Life rendering. Notice that I add formatting parameters to ensure that its different elements (e.g., Compass/Square, Cross) are visually distinct. One must have defined TOLpoints before using TOLpaths. I include another Mathematica built-in function, GeoCircle, used here for the first time. The reader is cautioned when attempting to use GeoCircle on a large Mercator projection, as it will differ from a hand-drawn circle on the same map, for reasons pertaining to the interpretation of distance.

```
TOLpaths[anchor_, θ_, scale_, pathtype_] := {
  Black, Thickness[Large], (* Center column, Cross *)
  GeoPath[{TOLpoints[anchor, θ, scale, pathtype][[1]],
    TOLpoints[anchor, θ, scale, pathtype][[10]]}, pathtype],
  GeoPath[{TOLpoints[anchor, θ, scale, pathtype][[2]],
    TOLpoints[anchor, θ, scale, pathtype][[3]]}, pathtype],
  Dashed, (* Compass / Square *)
  GeoPath[{TOLpoints[anchor, θ, scale, pathtype][[2]],
    TOLpoints[anchor, θ, scale, pathtype][[6]]}, pathtype],
  GeoPath[{TOLpoints[anchor, θ, scale, pathtype][[3]],
    TOLpoints[anchor, θ, scale, pathtype][[6]]}, pathtype],
  GeoPath[{TOLpoints[anchor, θ, scale, pathtype][[1]],
    TOLpoints[anchor, θ, scale, pathtype][[7]]}, pathtype],
  GeoPath[{TOLpoints[anchor, θ, scale, pathtype][[1]],
    TOLpoints[anchor, θ, scale, pathtype][[8]]}, pathtype],
  Thickness[Medium], Dashing[None], (* Pyramids *)
  GeoPath[{TOLpoints[anchor, θ, scale, pathtype][[6]],
    TOLpoints[anchor, θ, scale, pathtype][[7]]}, pathtype],
  GeoPath[{TOLpoints[anchor, θ, scale, pathtype][[6]],
    TOLpoints[anchor, θ, scale, pathtype][[8]]}, pathtype],
  GeoPath[{TOLpoints[anchor, θ, scale, pathtype][[7]],
```

```
   TOLpoints[anchor, θ, scale, pathtype][[10]]}, pathtype],
GeoPath[{TOLpoints[anchor, θ, scale, pathtype][[8]],
   TOLpoints[anchor, θ, scale, pathtype][[10]]}, pathtype],
GeoPath[{TOLpoints[anchor, θ, scale, pathtype][[7]],
   TOLpoints[anchor, θ, scale, pathtype][[9]]}, pathtype],
GeoPath[{TOLpoints[anchor, θ, scale, pathtype][[8]],
   TOLpoints[anchor, θ, scale, pathtype][[9]]}, pathtype],
GeoPath[{TOLpoints[anchor, θ, scale, pathtype][[14]],
   TOLpoints[anchor, θ, scale, pathtype][[7]]}, pathtype],
GeoPath[{TOLpoints[anchor, θ, scale, pathtype][[14]],
   TOLpoints[anchor, θ, scale, pathtype][[8]]}, pathtype],
Thickness[Tiny],(* cross connections *)
GeoPath[{TOLpoints[anchor, θ, scale, pathtype][[4]],
   TOLpoints[anchor, θ, scale, pathtype][[5]]}, pathtype],
GeoPath[{TOLpoints[anchor, θ, scale, pathtype][[7]],
   TOLpoints[anchor, θ, scale, pathtype][[8]]}, pathtype],
GeoPath[{TOLpoints[anchor, θ, scale, pathtype][[1]],
   TOLpoints[anchor, θ, scale, pathtype][[2]]}, pathtype],
GeoPath[{TOLpoints[anchor, θ, scale, pathtype][[1]],
   TOLpoints[anchor, θ, scale, pathtype][[3]]}, pathtype],
GeoPath[{TOLpoints[anchor, θ, scale, pathtype][[2]],
   TOLpoints[anchor, θ, scale, pathtype][[7]]}, pathtype],
GeoPath[{TOLpoints[anchor, θ, scale, pathtype][[3]],
   TOLpoints[anchor, θ, scale, pathtype][[8]]}, pathtype],
Thickness[Medium], (* Circle *)
GeoCircle[TOLpoints[anchor, θ, scale, pathtype][[6]]
}
```

Let's put a few of these tools together to plot the Tree of Life on Oak Island and extend its center column through the Newport Tower. We'll generate two plots, the first is a plot on Oak Island, and the second is a plot at the Newport Tower. I define two variables that capture the plot range I aim to display at Oak Island and Newport. They begin with gr. Lookup the GeoRange parameter to see how it works. Note that the GeoGraphics calls below only differ by their GeoRange, so the line coming out of the Oak Island Tree of Life center column is the same as the line passing through the Newport Tower.

```
datum = "ITRF00";
ftpm = 3.280839895;(*feet per meter*)
mpmi = 5280/ftpm;(*meters per mile*)
(*ptF from Amundsen*)
```

```
oakisland = GeoPosition[{FromDMS[{44,30,46.5864}],
  -FromDMS[{64,17,41.5134}]},datum];
groakisland = {{44.517290,44.509460},
  {-64.302623, -64.284507}};
OITOLpts := TOLpoints[oakisland, 59.540434, 1, "Rhumb"]
OITOLpath := TOLpaths[oakisland, 59.540434, 1, "Rhumb"]
nptower = GeoPosition[{41.485818, -71.309856}, datum];
grnptower = {{41.486415, 41.484792},
  {-71.310992, -71.307852}};
(* Oak Island graphic *)
GeoGraphics[{
  Point[OITOLpts], Point[nptower],
  OITOLpath,
  GeoCircle[nptower, 10/ftpm],(* Newport Tower *)
  Red, Dashed,
  geoextensionpath[OITOLpts[[1]],OITOLpts[[10]],
    420*mpmi*ftpm/1152,"Rhumb"]
  },
  GeoProjection -> "Mercator",
  GeoRange -> groakisland]
GeoGraphics[{
  Point[OITOLpts], Point[nptower],
  OITOLpath,
  GeoCircle[nptower, 10/ftpm],(* Newport Tower *)
  Red, Dashed,
  geoextensionpath[OITOLpts[[1]], OITOLpts[[10]],
    420*mpmi*ftpm/1152,"Rhumb"]
  },
  GeoProjection -> "Mercator",
  GeoRange -> grnptower]
```

You now possess the tools to use Mathematica to explore the technical elements of this investigation. Be certain to use rhumb lines, and to know when Mathematica might be defaulting to a geodesic line. You'll notice, as you step through these calculations, that judgment calls are necessary. For example, how does one define the exact point for Cedar Point, NC, which is the size of a small town? When I first discovered Cedar Point, NC, I chose a point on the beach due south of the GW MM. I later moved it because of another peculiar alignment, which I explained in the previous appendix. There are other spots that I could have chosen to make my -33, +33 alignments with the other Cedar Points more accurate, but I chose a spot that seemed consistent with the overall plan. In other words, be careful to avoid the desire to begin massaging the data to make it look better. Some error is to be expected, as this plan was laid out using hand tools and primitive maps. It is nonsense to expect modern accuracy and precision. Try achieving better than a half-degree of precision using a hand-drawn map and a protractor.

Here is some code that reveals the characteristics of Cedar Point, NC. It all begins with the Scottish Rite Temple in Charlotte, the Octagon House in Cedar Point, NC, and the Alexandria War Dead Monument. I chose the Alexandria War Dead Monument as the anchor, rather than the GW MM, because the War Dead Monument marks point [10] on the GW MM TOL and connects with the enlarged TOL in Washington DC (Figure 13).

```
datum = "ITRF00";
mpmi = 5280/ftpm; (* meters per mile *)
scottishritecharlotte = GeoPosition[{35.171947, -80.797307},
  datum];
alexandriawardeadmonument = GeoPosition[{38.806753,
  -77.062434, 10}, datum];
octagonhouseNC = GeoPosition[{34.686414, -77.086454},
  datum];
cedarpointNC = lineintersection[
  scottishritecharlotte,
  geoextensionpt[scottishritecharlotte, octagonhouseNC,
    1.2, "Rhumb"],
  alexandriawardeadmonument,
  geodestination[alexandriawardeadmonument, 300*mpmi,
    180, "Rhumb"],
  "Rhumb"];
oakisland = GeoPosition[{
  FromDMS[{44,30,46.5864}],
  -FromDMS[{64,17,41.5134}]},datum];
cedarpointOH = GeoPosition[{41.485818, -82.682355},
  datum];
cedarpointRI = GeoPosition[{41.404704, -71.493410},
  datum];
(* These lines without the ; are the output *)
geoazimuth[cedarpointNC, cedarpointOH, "Rhumb"]
geoazimuth[cedarpointNC, cedarpointRI, "Rhumb"]
geoazimuth[cedarpointNC, oakisland, "Rhumb"]
geoazimuth[octagonhouseNC,scottishritecharlotte,"Rhumb"]+360
```

The Pharaoh. I'll leave you with some code to contemplate. First, here is a function that returns a `GeoPath` from a given location toward a named star's rise or set azimuth, along a given pathtype.

```
starpath[loc_, dist_, starname_, event_, pathtype_] :=
   Module[{eventvar, mpmi, az},
     mpmi = 5280/3.280839895; (* give distance in miles *)
     If[event=="Rise", (* If not "Rise", then "Set" *)
       Eventvar = "AzimuthRise",
       eventvar = "AzimuthSet"];
     az = UnitConvert[
       StarData[starname,
         EntityProperty["Star",eventvar,{"Location"->loc}]],
       "AngularDegrees"];
     Print[az];
     GeoPath[{loc, dist*mpmi, az}, pathtype]
   ]
```

Now, let's graph the `GeoPath` to the setting of Betelgeuse, the bright star in Orion's shoulder, from point[10] of the GW MM TOL.

```
GWMMTOL10 = GeoPosition[{38.807055, -77.062436}, "ITRF00"];
GeoGraphics[{
  starpath[GWMMTOL10, .25, "Betelgeuse", "Set", "Rhumb"]
  },
  GeoProjection -> "Mercator",
  GeoRange -> 500,
  GeoCenter -> GWMMTOL10
]
```

The azimuth to this setting star at this location, according to Mathematica, is 279.984 degrees. What else at this location bears 279 degrees?

Sources

All photographs are the work of the author. All maps were generated using Mathematica v10.

The four sources of this book pertaining to Freemasonry and the Mysteries are in the public domain. Any quotes attributed to Pike, Wilmshurst, and Hall come from these books, except as footnoted in the text.

Pike, Albert. (1871) *Morals and Dogma*.

Wilmshurst, W.L. (1922) *The Meaning Of Masonry*.

Hall, Manly P. (1928) *The Secret Teachings of All Ages*.

Brown , Robert Hewitt. (1882) *Stellar Theology and Masonic Astronomy*.

Oak Island sources:

Amundsen, Petter. (2014) *Oak Island & the Treasure Map in Shakespeare*. Kindle Edition.

O'Connor, D'Arcy. (2004) *The Secret Treasure of Oak Island: The Amazing True Story of a Centuries-Old Treasure Hunt*. Lyons.

Crooker, William S. (2014) *Oak Island Gold*. Nimbus. Kindle Edition.

I used quotations from several translated texts.

Holy Bible: New International Version. (1984). International Bible Society.

The Bhagavad Gita (E. Easwaran trans.). (1985). Nigiri Press.

Alighieri, Dante. (1954) *The Divine Comedy* (J. Ciardi trans.). NAL.

The Koran (N.J. Dawood trans). (1985). Penguin Classics.

Lao-Tzu. (1990) *Tao Te Ching* (V.H. Mair trans.). Bantam Books.

For information on the Qabalah and Buddhism, I primarily used:

Parfitt, Will. (1999) *The Elements of The Qabalah*. Barnes & Noble.

Batchelor, Stephen. (1997) *Buddhism Without Beliefs*. Riverhead.

Mathers, S.L. MacGregor. (1887) *The Kabbalah Unveiled*. Kessinger.

These websites were helpful: www.wikipedia.com, www.kingjamesbibleonline.org, www.gwmemorial.org, www.alexandriava.gov.

About the Author

Façade

Don't be fooled by the
    chrysanthemums

on your left as you come through the
    door.
They've kept well without much
    light,

and I am still the
perfect
    stranger.

- Adam Schneider

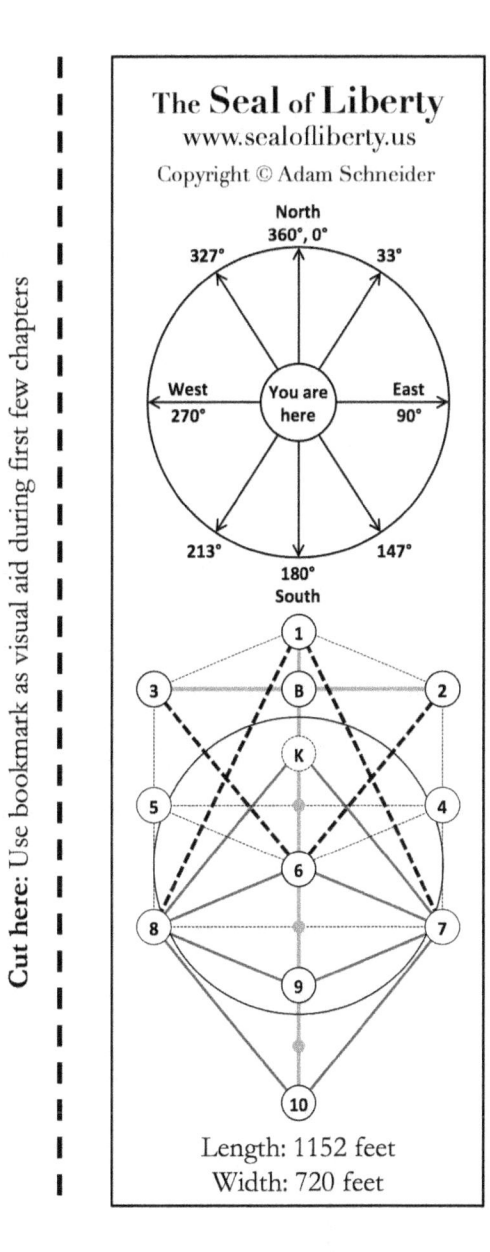

North
360°, 0°
327°   33°
West   East
270°   90°
You are here
213°   147°
180°
South

Length: 1152 feet
Width: 720 feet